BOOKS BY HY BRETT

A SECRET REPORT TO THE TRUE
AMERICAN FAITH SOCIETY:
Senior Citizens and Their Threat to America

HOW TO SURVIVE THE NEW MILLENNIUM:
Recycled Wisdom for an Age of Diminished Expectations

THE ULTIMATE NEW YORK CITY TRIVIA

A BOOK OF LOVE FOR MY SON
Co-Authored with H. Jackson Brown

PROMISES TO KEEP
Co-Authored with Barbara Brett

Wishful Weddings

From *Casablanca* to *Titanic*…
Star-Crossed Lovers United at Last!

Hy Brett

For Barbara

How delicious is the winning
Of a kiss at love's beginning,
When two mutual hearts are sighing
For the knot there's no untying!
Thomas Campbell

PREFACE

Whenever I attend a wedding and observe the exultation of the bride and groom, I am compelled to take out a handkerchief and shed a tear for all the characters in books, plays and films who never quite made it to the altar. I think, for example, of *The Maltese Falcon*, in which private eye Sam Spade had to be professional and pin the murder of his partner, Miles Archer, on the lovely and amorous Brigid O'Shaughnessy. We have all heard that absence makes the heart grow fonder, but, on the other hand, forty years in Alcatraz may well chill a relationship between a man and a woman.

This book reverses the marital decisions of writers who were ruled by their heads and not their hearts. If any readers can show just cause why these characters may not lawfully be joined together, let them now speak or else forever hold their peace. Foreseeing criticism from folks who have suffered vertigo on the marriage-go-round, I admit at once that only God and maybe Yente, the matchmaker in *Fiddler on the Roof*, can know for sure whether my brides and grooms would have been better off if they had married someone else. Or if, Cupid forbid, they had remained single. However, to make these unions more official and respectable, here are the wedding notices as they would have appeared in local newspapers, whether *The New York Times*, *The Madison County Livestock Gazette*, *The Wuthering Heights Evening Breeze*, *The Metropolis Daily Planet*, *The Elsinore Castle Herald-Chronicle*, *The Verona Courier*, *The Skull Island Post-Mortem Enquirer*, or *The Duchy of Frankenstein Herald*.

In several of the notices, the brides and grooms are characters whose loves and longings were, for some reason, ignored by their authors, and I have attempted to correct these shameful oversights.

CONTENTS

CASABLANCA

ILSA LUND LASZLO AND RICHARD S. BLAINE

Ilsa Lund Laszlo, the daughter of the late Mr. and Mrs. Frederick Lund of Prague, was married yesterday in Washington, D.C., to Richard S. Blaine, son of the late Stanley and Penelope Blaine of Chicago. The ceremony was performed at St. Theresa's Church by Bishop Louis Haville of Marseilles. Bishop Haville, a former major in the French army, was stationed in the early '40s in Casablanca, Morocco, where the groom owned Rick's Place, a night club and gambling casino, until it was confiscated by the German authorities after the airport slaying of their local commandant, Gen. Fritz von Sheller.

Mrs. Blaine, 42, is the widow of Victor Laszlo, a leader in the European underground struggle against the Nazi invaders during the worst years of World War II. Mr. Laszlo's health was permanently impaired in the course of his day and night labors, but he lived long enough to witness the liberation of Europe. General Dwight D. Eisenhower, Prime Minister Winston

Churchill and General Charles de Gaulle were among the comrades in arms who attended his funeral in Prague on April 16, 1946. Since the end of the war and her distinguished service in the underground, Mrs. Blaine has been a media consultant at Shlick, Wetz and Grundig, an advertising agency in Prague. She graduated from the University of Bohemia, where she majored in cryptography and espionage.

Mr. Blaine, 55, postponed his studies at Northwestern University to pursue business opportunities as a professional gambler both at home and abroad. During a poker game in Casablanca, he won the establishment that he renamed Rick's Place, and he operated it for six years until he and Father Haville fled to occupied France, where they led the underground until Mr. Blaine was appointed by President Roosevelt to help establish the O.S.S., an overseas intelligence network that later became the C.I.A., of which he is presently assistant director. The wedding march, by Felix Mendelssohn, was performed with grandeur and solemnity on the church organ by Sam Cook, an old friend of the groom, and once his pianist at Rick's Place in Casablanca. At the reception later on, in Mr. Cook's night club in Georgetown, Rick's Place II, he played "As Time Goes By" on his old piano. The bride and groom agreed that the song had a multitude of memories for them, almost as many as the lid of Sam's old piano had rings from their glasses of wine and whiskey.

They will honeymoon in Monte Carlo, where Mr. Blaine intends to play roulette and win possession of the world-famous casino, which will become Rick and Ilsa's Place.

ROMEO AND JULIET

JULIET CAPULET AND ROMEO MONTAGUE

Juliet Capulet, the sheltered daughter of Lord and Lady Capulet of fair Verona, was married yesterday to Romeo Montague, the ardent and impetuous son of Lord and Lady Montague, also of Verona. After a special dispensation from His Holiness the Pope, the ceremony was performed at the Church of the Annunciation by Friar Lawrence, who until now has restricted his duties to prayer and premarital counseling. Originally, both the bride and groom had expressed a strong desire for a moonlight ceremony on their very special spot, the balcony outside her bedchamber that offers a splendid but inconstant view of the moon. But when they and Friar Lawrence and their immediate families all stepped out upon it for a rehearsal, it immediately crashed to the ground. Rushed to Verona for his estimate of the damage, Papal architect Michelangelo Buonarroti said that a new balcony of equal beauty could not possibly be built in time for the nuptial day. If the balcony was really a must, he suggested that they postpone the wedding for ten years, when he should be finished with his painting of the Sistine Chapel.

The bride, 14, studied singing, flirting and gossiping with her nurse, and then learned aristocratic deportment and household supervision from her mother, Lady Maria Capulet, whose ancestors fought in the crusades to free Jerusalem from the infidels, and later introduced the pastry called Turkish delight to Italy. The ancestry of Lord Capulet is no less distinguished, and it was a fourteenth-century member of the Venetian branch of the family, Lord Luciano Capulet, who introduced the famous watercraft that still bears the name of his beloved wife, the Lady Gondola of Milan.

Romeo, 19, who is majoring in falconry at the University of Turin, studied fencing with his friend Mercutio until the latter was killed in a street brawl with Tybalt, a kinsman of Mrs. Juliet Montague. When Romeo killed Tybalt in revenge, he was banished by the Duke until Lord Enrico Montague, Romeo's father, reminded the Duke that he had once saved him from drinking from a poisoned bottle of Chianti '56, a gift from the vineyards of Lucretia Borgia. A gentleman of honor who can trace his ancestry back to King Priam of ancient Troy, the Duke returned the favor and pardoned Romeo on condition that he and the other Montagues forever after keep the public peace with the Capulets.

The wedding reception had just begun when Juliet's old nurse was hurried away to her quarters. Already tipsy, she was singing a ditty to the effect that her former charge might become a mother in far fewer than the customary nine months after a nuptial night.

THE BARBIE AND KEN DOLL COLLECTION

BARBIE DOLL AND KEN DOLL

Barbara Ellen Doll, a daughter of Raggedy Andy and Raggedy Ann Doll of the R. H. Macy toy department in New York City, was married yesterday to her distant cousin, Kenneth Spencer Doll, a son of G.I. Joe and G.I. Josephine Doll of the Toys R Us store in the White Mountain Shopping Center in Fordham, New Hampshire. The Rev. J. Peter Penguin performed the ceremony at the Church of St. Germayne, the guardian of children, in Staten Island. The Rev. Penguin, a family friend of both sets of parents, was so exhausted by his long swim from his official parish in Antarctica that he had to be restuffed completely at the As Good As New Doll Hospital in Brooklyn.

Mrs. Doll graduated cum laude from the La Reine de Beauté School of Modeling in Manhattan and is currently the most popular model with the Jessica Windsor Agency. Thanks to her exquisite appearance in a variety of hairstyles and wardrobes, she has appeared on the cover and also on the pages of such important magazines as *Cosmopolitan, Vogue, Harper's Bazaar, Elle* and the annual swimwear edition of *Sports Illustrated.* Endowed with anatomical correctness, she has sought to share her blessings with women of all ages, and her exercise videos, endorsed by celebrities and Olympic champions, now outsell all others.

Mr. Doll attended Toyland University on an athletic scholarship until he badly twisted an arm during the fourth quarter of a football game against The Plaything Institute of Technology. While he was recuperating at Massachusetts General Doll Hospital in Boston, a fellow patient who happened to be a fashion photographer was much impressed by his appearance in a striped orange bathrobe and a pair of blue silk pajamas with yellow hearts. His picture of Mr. Doll appeared on the cover of a J. C. Penney catalogue, and Mr. Doll has been the world's preeminent male model ever since.

Aware that their wedding would be the most important event in their life, Mr. and Mrs. Doll ordered not only a wedding gown and formal evening attire for the church ceremony and reception, but also a complete outfit for the trip from their homes to the church, and another complete outfit from the reception to Newark Airport, where they would be departing for their ten-day honeymoon in Hawaii. Employing six trunks and twenty-two suitcases, all color-coordinated, they have already forwarded the three hundred garments of their fun-in-the-sun ensembles to the Hawaii Hilton. In order to accommodate their clothes as well as themselves, they had to book the Pineapple Suite and also rent three portable wardrobes from BobbieHannahMontanaDollhouses.com.

THE BRIDGES OF MADISON COUNTY

FRANCESCA JOHNSON AND
ROBERT KINCAID

Francesca Johnson, a daughter of the late Antonio and Maria Mancuso of Scudari, a village near Bologna, was married yesterday to Robert Kincaid, the prize-winning photographer whose works are in the permanent collections of the International Center of Photography and other famous museums. The Rev. Andrew Legato, the bride's parish priest in Madison County, Iowa, performed the ceremony at the Church of Santa Maria dei Miracoli in Venice.

The bride, 55, received her education in Christian morality and also secular subjects at the St. Filumena School in Scudari, and she won there many prizes for her preparation of carrots and pasta primavera. One of her essays, entitled "Can Sophia Loren Be a Role Model for a Catholic Girl?" was commended by her Mother Superior and printed in the *Scudari Messenger*.

After a previous marriage to Richard Johnson, an American soldier, and then her relocation in Madison

County, the bride's cannolis and zeppolis were much admired at bake sales in the area, and she appeared briefly but memorably in a segment of *On the Road*, the popular TV series hosted by Charles Kuralt. Mr. Johnson died heroically two years ago, while directing rescue operations during the worst flood of the North Raccoon River in over a century. In appreciation of his long service both to humans and animals, the Iowa Cattlemen's Association awarded season passes to home games of the Madison Marvels to his widow and their two children, Carolyn and Michael.

The bridegroom, 62, dropped out during his sophomore year at Northwestern University, but later graduated with honors from the Chicago Institute of Photography. Though invited to teach at his alma mater, he preferred to work at his craft, especially outdoors. His world-famous photographs of the covered bridges in Madison County, Iowa, which first appeared in *The National Geographic* in 1966, were so popular with both critics and the public that Eastman Kodak appointed him as its official photographer and roving ambassador of goodwill. He was successful in both capacities, producing not only a spate of pictorial masterpieces but also being honored as Man of the Decade by the National Association of Farm Wives. On the twenty-fifth anniversary of his trip to Madison County, the

Italian-American Arts Council commissioned him to photograph the equally famous bridges over the canals in Venice. It was while he was photographing the Bridge of Sighs that he reencountered the former Mrs. Johnson, whom he had known briefly back in Madison County. She was in Venice to attend the funeral of an aunt, and also, if possible, to find new low-calorie recipes for her bake sales.

The couple will honeymoon in Paris, where, combining business with romance, the groom will photograph the bridges over the Seine for a special travel edition of *Modern Maturity* magazine.

THE LASSIE AND BENJI MOVIES

LASSIE AND BENJI

Lassie, a daughter of Mr. Pal and Mrs. Princess of Harrison Heights, Missouri, was married yesterday afternoon to Benji, a son of Ms. Ginger of Chicago and of an unknown father, either of Chicago or of Las Vegas, where Mr. and Mrs. John Styles, the family with whom the groom's mother resides, frequently visit for relaxation. Ms. Georgina Stewart, a longtime judge at the Ozark Dog Show, performed the civil ceremony at the Windsor Kennel Club in St. Louis.

The bride, 3, majored in obedience at Laura Laverne's Institute for Classy Canines in Darlington, and she later graduated with honors from the Hale Carnegie School of Deportment and Communication Skills. She has appeared on TV commercials for Purina dog foods and Trump kennels. Also, fulfilling her responsibilities as man's best friend, she is affiliated with both the police and the fire departments in Columbia County, and has been cited by local and state officials for her heroic rescues of creatures great and small, and regardless of their race, religion, national origin, breed, or species.

The bridegroom, 4, studied the retrieving of balls and sticks at the Young Men and Dogs' Christian Association of Chicago. His proficiency brought him to the attention of Hal Gruder, manager of the Chicago Cubs, and he was appointed mascot of the team. While the Cubs were playing in Busch Stadium in St. Louis, a thief stole the favorite bat of outfielder Ned DeLuis, and the bridegroom's investigation led him to Columbia County, where he and Ms. Lassie were able to combine their skills and apprehend the thief.

The bride's father retired last year as dean of street-crossing studies at the Missouri Seeing Eye Dog College, but her mother continues to serve with the Narcotics Inspection Service at St. Louis Airport. During the first course of the dinner at McKibble's restaurant that followed the ceremony, a cocker spaniel named Mr. Rover leaped through the window and identified himself as the father of the groom. The groom's mother suspected that Mr. Rover was more interested in the refreshments than in family values, but after sniffing him thoroughly and then biting his tail, she agreed to let him stay and to reestablish a tentative and platonic relationship with her.

THE MALTESE FALCON

BRIGID O'SHAUGHNESSY AND SAMUEL SPADE

After all present had imbibed a slug of bootleg whiskey for good luck, Brigid Cecile Kathleen O'Shaughnessy, who claims descent from the kings of Ireland but whose immediate antecedents are Spike and Babe O'Shaughnessy of Brooklyn, New York, was married yesterday to Samuel Donald Spade, the son of Lucille and Nicholas Spade, who reside on the wrong side of the tracks in Laguna Junction, a suburb of San Francisco. Judge Richard M. Dugan, who had once sentenced Mrs. Spade to twenty-five years at hard labor at Alcatraz, performed the ceremony in his chambers at the Criminal Courts Building in San Francisco.

Even after her incarceration at Alcatraz, Mrs. Spade still claimed to be innocent in the death of, among other alleged victims, Miles Archer, Mr. Spade's partner in a detective agency on Bush Street. At various times she claimed that the murder had been committed by an Oriental hit woman who called herself The Dutchman in order to fool the authorities, or by a trained falcon from Malta. Her sentence was eventually shortened to two years after Warden Edward Gluck wrote a glowing report on her improvement in conduct, due in part to his personal counseling after slugs of Jack Daniels in his private office.

Mr. Spade, who received his master's degree from the Chuck Collins Correspondence School of Criminal Detection, has turned down repeated offers to head the Federal Bureau of Investigation in Washington, because he believes that it is impossible to get a decent bowl of chop suey away from San Francisco's Chinatown. Upon his engagement last month to the former Miss O'Shaughnessy, Mr. Spade came to a mutual understanding with Effie Perine, his longtime gal Friday. They agreed wholeheartedly that, considering Mrs. Spade's prowess with firearms, their present relationship was not really going anywhere except maybe to the morgue.

Depending on the relative quality of the chop suey and bootleg gin, Mr. and Mrs. Spade will honeymoon in either Atlantic City or Niagara Falls.

CARMEN

CARMEN DEL RIO AND
DON JOSÉ LOPEZ Y MURILLO

After a long and tempestuous courtship that included stabbing and defenestration, Carmen del Rio, a gypsy of obscure parentage, was married yesterday to Don José Lopez y Murillo, son of Armando and Maria Theresa Lopez of the Basque province in Spain. Msgr. Michael Kelly officiated at All Saints Church in East Harlem in New York City.

The groom's parents, landowners who can trace their ancestry to the conquistadores who rid Spain of the Moors in the fifteenth century, did not attend the ceremony. They disapprove so strongly of their son's marriage to a gypsy without even a single drop of noble blood in her veins that they have appealed to the Pope to annual the marriage on the grounds that she is still married in Spain to at least six other men, all commoners as well as common criminals.

Mrs. Lopez, 31, majored in purse-snatching and pocket-picking at the Gypsy Baron Academy of Arts and Science, a non-accredited institution in Seville. After graduating with honors, she interrupted a flourishing career to spend two years at the San Vinden Reformatory for Wayward Girls in Barcelona. Upon being paroled from that establishment, she found honest daytime employment as a cigarette processor at Casa Marlboro, a tobacco company in Seville. Her nights, however, were devoted to prostitution, drinking brandy, and other pursuits congenial to her gypsy heritage and nature.

Mr. Lopez, 32, graduated as a lieutenant of cavalry from the King Ferdinand Military Academy in Murillo. After saving the former Miss del Rio from arrest for the stabbing of a colleague at the cigarette factory, he fell passionately in love with her, forsook his sacred responsibilities to his regiment, Spain and king, and then followed her into a life of banditry that included smuggling and even murder.

From time to time, especially at Easter and Christmas, his better nature warned him that he was living a life of evil, and he would implore Mrs. Lopez to start a new life with him in one of the new Hispanic communities in America. Eventually, with the aid of a monk named Brother Ernesto, she acceded to his requests, and they forged American immigration papers, robbed their last bank, and departed for their new and more virtuous life in New York City. He made her promise that if the streets there were really paved with gold, she would not attempt to steal them.

The newlyweds will honeymoon in Atlantic City. Upon their return to East Harlem, Mr. Lopez will resume his duties as a sergeant in the Cavalry Division of the New York Police Department, and Mrs. Lopez will realize a longtime dream in her new homeland of opportunity, and open a gypsy tea shop on Third Avenue, directly opposite Bloomingdale's, the world-famous department store. At the tea shop, her fortune-telling will specialize in turbulent romance and avoiding arrest.

WUTHERING HEIGHTS

CATHERINE E. LINTON AND HEATHCLIFF WALPOLE

Catherine Earnshaw Linton, the daughter of James and Amelia Earnshaw, both of them deceased and no doubt happy to be far away from her and her passions, was married last evening to Heathcliff Walpole, the natural son of the late Sir Robert Walpole and of Cherry James, a buxom chambermaid at the Primrose and Daisy, an inn near Lower Toople in Lincolnshire. The Rev. Silas Brock performed the ceremony at Wuthering Heights, the bride's ancestral home in the West Riding of Yorkshire. Of the thirteen people invited to the ceremony, only the groom's mother was able to attend. The others perished along the road during a sudden snowstorm from the Scottish highlands. The Rev. Brock refused to speculate whether the snowstorm was instigated by a witch who had once placed Wuthering Heights under a curse for all eternity.

Mrs. Walpole, 29, studied embroidery, drawing, singing and French with a succession of foreign and domestic tutors, all of whom went out one day for a healthful stroll across the moors and were never seen again. According to the Royal Yorkshire Constabulary, such was also the fate last year of Mr. Edgar Linton, the bride's former husband.

Mr. Walpole, 32, studied the agricultural arts and sciences with the late Andy Jenkins, a farmhand at Wuthering Heights. Shortly after the marriage of the former Miss Earnshaw, an unattainable childhood sweetheart, to the wealthy Mr. Linton, a childhood enemy, Mr. Walpole, then a foundling without a surname, antecedents or prospects, departed in a hailstorm to seek his name and make his fortune in London. There, deep in the archives of Somerset House, he learned that he was a direct, though illegitimate, descendant of Sir Robert Walpole, the Earl of Orford, who was twice prime minister during the reign of King George II. This distinguished lineage entitled Mr. Walpole to a generous credit line at the Royal Bank for Impecunious Bastards of the Peerage, and with an initial capital of only a thousand guineas, he quickly became a millionaire after cornering the market in both Spanish onions and roulette wheels from France.

The newlyweds will postpone their honeymoon until after next week's session of the Court of Libel and Slander in York Royal. The groom is currently suing the proprietor of *The West Murdoch Enquirer*, which has hinted in a front-page story, headlined A LOW BLOW AT WUTHERING HEIGHTS?, that there might be more than coincidence in his return to the scene of his juvenile turmoil and the disappearance the very next day of the husband of his childhood sweetheart. His solicitor, Sir Sylvester Moynes KC, denies emphatically the local rumors that the ghost of his client's predecessor, Edgar Linton, has been haunting the room that will be the nuptial bedchamber at Wuthering Heights.

THE CATCHER IN THE RYE

JEAN GALLAGHER AND HOLDEN CAULFIELD

Jean Gallagher, a daughter of Mr. and Mrs. Ernest Gallagher of Ipswich, Massachusetts, was married yesterday afternoon to Holden Caulfield, the son of Mr. and Mrs. Parker Caulfield of New York City and Martha's Vineyard. The Rev. Alex T. Merrill performed the ceremony at the Church of the Postmodernist Awakening in New York City. On Tuesdays and Thursdays for the past eighteen years, the bride and groom have been meeting at the Palm Court of the Plaza Hotel to critique and deconstruct their sessions of psychoanalysis with Dr. Alice Shapiro-Goldberg and Dr. Myron X. Burke, respectively. They decided to be married by the Rev. Merrill after dropping in at his church to hear a Sunday morning sermon entitled "Marriage—Can It Be More Than Just a Crap Shoot?" Still undecided about marriage after the sermon, they questioned the reverend's four former wives, who happened to be present to collect their alimony checks. The four women agreed that, despite the inevitable disagreements about the merits of Starbuck's coffee and suchlike important matters, marriage was still worth a try, especially with no-fault divorce and the abundance of excellent divorce lawyers in town. Their current husbands were playing softball in Central Park and unavailable for comment.

The bride, 39, will be keeping her own name unless it turns out to be too much of a hassle when she and the groom fill out their income tax returns. She graduated from Vassar College, where she was captain of the tiddledywinks team. The team never won a single match during her leadership, but was frequently cited for its sincerity by the American Existential Society. She received a master's degree in ethnology from Northwestern University, and is the founder and CEO of Looks Ain't Everything, a computerized dating service. Her firm is currently being sued for malpractice by a client who claims that while he was still on his honeymoon, the value of his wife's securities dropped by fully twenty-three percent and never recovered.

The groom, 40, attended Pencey Prep until he left in his junior year to embark on a course of independent study, specializing in contemporary American values and interpersonal relationships. Eventually, to please his parents, he resumed his formal education and graduated from the Quo Vadis Nonsectarian Talmud

Torah in Lower Manhattan, which was the closest school to Chinatown and its restaurants, where he was conducting a study of the effects of egg rolls upon the stability and happiness of both oriental and occidental families. His appearance in his red hunting hat on the cover of the annual men's fashion supplement of *Better Chinese Noodles and Wontons* led to modeling assignments and a position of fashion consultant to Forever 18, the men's clothing chain that caters to the young at heart of all ages.

Upon returning from their honeymoon in a secret location not far from an eatery with allegedly the best tiramisu in New England, Ms. Gallagher and Mr. Caulfield will be co-hosts on a new radio talk show for teenagers. Among their sponsors will be the Let There Be Sunshine Foundation, which counsels teenagers on the pros and cons of living beyond the age of twenty-five, and the Upper West Side Nightshade Society, producer of publications that assist would-be suicides.

FRANKENSTEIN

ELSA THE MONSTER AND
BORIS THE MONSTER

Elsa the Monster, the creation of Baron Dr. Victor von Frankenstein, was married yesterday to Boris the Monster, also created by Baron Dr. von Frankenstein, in the parlor of Castle Frankenstein in the midst of the Black Forest in Bavaria. Pastor Johann Leiber performed the Lutheran ceremony with the approval of Bishop Hans Husted, who had declared after consultation with a special synod that the union of the unusual bride and groom, created by the same scientist in the same laboratory, did not violate any church rulings on the sin of incest.

Elsa, 13 months old, is currently a maid to the Baroness Miritza von Frankenstein, but after hearing her mistress perform a piano transcription of "Invitation to the Dance," by her kinsman Carl Maria von Weber, she has expressed an interest in studying ballet. Because her legs once belonged to a woman with incipient arthritis, which may hinder her career on the stage, Baron Dr.

von Frankenstein is currently treating her with a new analgesic and anti-inflammatory medication that he originally called Alpspirin, in honor of the ski resort in the Swiss Alps where he and the Baroness have so often found spiritual as well as physical benefits. After learning that the name was unavailable for commercial use, he changed it to Aspirin.

Boris, who recently celebrated his second birthday, is a caretaker on the Frankenstein estate, and not a crow or poacher has been seen since he assumed his duties. Due to the incompetence of a laboratory assistant, who has since been discharged, Boris was furnished with the brain of Fritz Schultz, a homicidal maniac, but the Baron has been treating him temporarily with an experimental sedative of his own creation, called Lozak in honor of a former colleague and dueling partner at the University of Budapest. His Highness, King Frederick of Prussia, who anticipates another war with France or Austria or both, has offered Boris a commission as lieutenant in the Royal Uhlans.

The belated wedding presents of the Baron and Baroness von Frankenstein to Boris and Elsa will be, as soon as they are available from respectable donors in a consecrated cemetery, a new brain and a new pair of legs, respectively.

HAMLET, PRINCE OF DENMARK

OPHELIA AND HAMLET

Ophelia, the daughter of the late Polonius, Lord Chamberlain of Denmark until he was stabbed behind an arras by an unknown assailant, possibly a Lapp terrorist, was married yesterday to Prince Hamlet, son of the late King Hamlet and of Queen Gertrude, and stepson of the late King Claudius, who died of a stroke while attending a fencing match last month. His eminence, the Bishop of Copenhagen, performed the ceremony in the banqueting room of the royal castle in Elsinore, after which the company partook of baked meats, most of them left over from previous social occasions.

Princess Ophelia, 16, was tutored in the graces by Dr. Pretorius Luxis of the University of Hennesstein, and she is famed throughout Scandinavia for her gentle disposition and knowledge of botany, both its science and poetic lore. Her slim volume, *A Pansy for Your Thoughts*, was recently commended by Hedvig Schluff in *The Copenhagen Review of Books*. The princess enjoys a hoax from time to time, and though she is a backstroke champion and has swum the English Channel, among other waterways, she will upon occasion pretend to have drowned in a shallow pond or stream.

Prince Hamlet, 31, graduated from the University of Wittenberg, where he double majored in dramatics and public administration. He and Horatio, his best man at the wedding, were co-captains of the fencing team that won the European Collegiate Championship for two successive years.

Immediately after the wedding ceremony, Queen Gertrude announced her abdication and retirement to the nunnery of the Little Sisters of St. Helene, where she will devote herself to prayer, repentance and good works. Prince Hamlet and Princess Ophelia will be crowned when they return from their honeymoon in Paris, where Prince Hamlet, combining business of state with conjugal pleasure, will present King Louis the Fat with baskets of assorted low-calorie Danish, a pastry created in the king's honor by the court baker at Elsinore.

In accordance with the terms of his visa from the World Beyond, the ghost of Prince Hamlet's father was forced to leave the wedding before the banquet, but he promised the newlyweds that he will move heaven and earth to return for the complete christening ceremony of their firstborn and all subsequent offspring.

SUPERMAN COMICS AND MOVIES

LOIS LANE AND SUPERMAN

Lois Nancy Lane, star reporter on *The Daily Planet*, was married yesterday to Superman, a veteran superhero who has dedicated his strength and other unique abilities to the preservation of Truth, Justice and The American Way.

Mrs. Superman, 26, is the daughter of Beverly and Stephen Lane of Cambridge, Massachusetts. Both of Mrs. Superman's parents were full professors at Harvard, and they could well have afforded to give her a generous weekly allowance, but they preferred her to become as independent as their ancestors who had come over on the Mayflower, and so they suggested to her that she deliver newspapers every morning before attending classes at the Talbott School. One day she opened one of her newspapers and glanced at a sports story about her school before hurling it upon a porch. She was so shocked by the inaccuracies that, encouraged by Mrs. Brenda Starr Radcliffe, her neighbor, mentor and role model, she composed a more accurate account of the ballgame in a letter to the editor. The editor was so impressed by her zeal and ability that he immediately offered her a job as cub reporter. She postponed accepting his offer for three years, until she had graduated magna cum laude from the School of Journalism at the University of Missouri.

Her rapid rise from cub reporter in Boston to star reporter at the Daily Planet in Metropolis is legendary in the profession, and she has rejected frequent offers from media mogul Rupert Murdoch to head either *The New York Post* or *The Wall Street Journal*, and from CBS-TV to head *Sixty Minutes* and from MSNBC to replace Rachel Maddow.

Mr. Superman, 32 in earth years, is the only son of the late Erga and Maximo, both senior intergalactic advisers on the planet Krypton until its destruction. Not only individuals but also cities and whole nations, including the United States of America, owe their very existence to the selfless activities of Mr. Superman, and, if necessary, he will, at a moment's notice, postpone his personal engagements and leap across the ocean to rescue a child from a Paris sewer or a kitten from a tree in London's Hyde Park.

Mr. Superman's best man at the wedding ceremony, performed by the Rev. Liz Hammon at the First Episcopal Church in Cambridge, was to have been Clark Kent, Mrs. Superman's mild-mannered colleague at *The Daily Planet*, but he was called away at the last minute to write a breaking story about a Coney Island hot-dog eating contest in which Nathan's, the sponsor, ran out of hot dogs while the two finalists were still going strong after having each consumed 56. Mr. Kent forgot to leave behind the wedding ring before he left for Coney Island. But within a minute of his departure it was delivered by Mr. Batman of Gotham City. A fellow superhero and also longtime friend of Mr. Superman, he was delighted to substitute as best man.

Within minutes of the end of the gala reception at the Lane residence, Mr. and Mrs. Superman arrived at the Ritz Hotel in Paris, the first stop in their three-week honeymoon unless they are called back to Metropolis to write up a big story or correct a gross miscarriage of justice.

A CHRISTMAS CAROL

FANNY MARLEY AND SIR EBENEZER SCROOGE

Fanny Marley, the daughter of the late Mr. and Mrs. Silas Welles of Dumley on the Severn, was married yesterday in London to Sir Ebenezer Scrooge, the son of the late Mr. and Mrs. Andrew Scrooge of Dover. The Rev. Robert Worthington performed the ceremony at St. Martin's in the Strand, which recently received both a new organ and carillon from one of the groom's many philanthropies, the Scrooge Foundation for the Preservation of Church Music.

Lady Fanny, 55, is the widow of the late Jacob Marley, a partner in the factoring firm of Scrooge and Marley, which was sold last year to the Buddenbrooks Group so that Sir Ebenezer could devote himself completely to his philanthropies. Lady Fanny studied cooking and baking with her mother, once a kitchen maid at Buckingwald, the estate of the Duke of Devon, and she was famous throughout Putney for her brownies and ginger snaps.

Sir Ebenezer, 60, was elevated in the Queen's Honor List two years ago, not, as is the custom, on New Year's Day, but on Christmas, a day that will always be associated with Sir Ebenezer and his benevolence to Londoners, Britain and the whole empire. After an estrangement since the death of the late Mr. Marley, Sir Ebenezer and his bride-to-be met again last Easter Day at the grave of Mr. Marley in Hampstead Cemetery. Appalled by the knowledge that his late partner, because of his parsimony and greed, had been sentenced by the Deity to spend eternity in chains, Sir Ebenezer had, upon his own enlightenment, established the Jacob Marley Memorial Fund for the Relief of Widows, Orphans and Homeless Animals. At the grave on Easter, while the visitors were reminiscing about the departed, an apparition of Mr. Marley arose from the ground. He was smiling, and without chains, and he thanked Sir Ebenezer for his liberation, and he said that his happiness in heaven would be complete if his two visitors could be united in holy matrimony.

Sir Ebenezer and Lady Fanny will honeymoon on the Island of Harris, where they will distribute geese and shillings to the population, which has been hard hit by the drop in price of their tweed cloth. They will be attended by their factotum, Timothy "Tiny Tim" Cratchit, whose corrective surgery at the Scrooge Free

Hospital in Chelsea enabled him to reach a height of six feet and go on to become heavyweight boxing champion of the British Empire.

APPROVED FOR PUBLICATION BY THE
IMPERIAL MINISTRY OF JUSTICE AND
INCARCERATION

CRIME AND PUNISHMENT

SONIA VEREFSKAYA AND
RODION RASKOLNIKOV

Sonia Verefskaya, of unknown parentage and raised in the orphanage of the Little Mothers of Charity in St. Petersburg, was married yesterday in the Queen Alexandra Rehabilitation Camp in Utsk, Siberia, to Rodion Raskolnikov, the son of Masha Raskolnikova and of the late Grigor Ivanov Raskolnikov of Moxuk, a hamlet two hundred versts from Moscow as the imperial eagle flies. The bride's orphanage, dedicated to the glory of God and the House of Romanov, was established in 1322 by Czar Ivan the Terrible, who was always merciful to widows and orphans and terrible only to enemies of his dynasty and Holy Mother Russia. The groom's father was treasurer of Moxuk for many years. When he succumbed to a fit of sneezing during a procession in honor of a visit from Prince Andrei, he was so disgraced that he soon resigned his position and drank himself to death with Old Sascha, a thrift brand of vodka intended only for external use after whippings and suchlike minor skin conditions.

Father Semyon, chaplain of Section 2,003 in the correctional facility, officiated at the traditional Orthodox service in the chapel dedicated to the glory of St. Vladimir and the House of Romanov. The facility is one of the most modern and comfortable in Siberia if not in the whole Empire, with crucifixes, Bibles, icons, and pictures of the Czar and Czarina in every cell, even those devoted to solitary confinement. Outdoors, there is a plentitude of barbed wire for the discouragement of unscheduled exits, which always lead to unscheduled encounters with wolves, tigers and polar bears.

The bride, 20, learned her catechism and the domestic arts and sciences at the orphanage. She was especially proficient in peeling potatoes and preparing turnips and carrots for the daily bowl of soup that was decreed by Czar Ivan in his charter for the orphanage, and it was while she was hurrying along Princess Oblomsky Avenue, on her way to impart her skills to a sister institution where the carrot and turnip tops were not being trimmed properly that she met her husband to be. Together, disregarding their haste, they bent over and raised Raisa Khromonovna, a great-grandmother of seventeen souls who had been struck down in the snow by a hit-and-run troika whose driver was on his way to St. Igor's Church to confess his sexual misbehavior with his serfs.

Mr. Raskolnikov, 24, was a philosophy student, majoring in ethics and metaphysics, at St. Petersburg University until he discontinued regular attendance in order to save laundry bills and also devote himself in his cold room to pondering the existence of God and the purpose of man's existence on earth, especially in Holy Mother Russia. He had just come away from murdering an avaricious pawnbroker in an attempt to prove to himself that his keen intellect had enabled him to free himself from the moral prohibitions of God and the legal system that interprets and validates the infallible wisdom of the Czar. The simple faith and unselfish deeds of Sonia, his new acquaintance, set Rodion upon a course of self-examination that led him to confess his crime to Police Inspector Porfiry and to view his punishment of twenty-five years imprisonment as a blessing in disguise that, with the Czar's inspiration and Sonia's help, he would one day be able to understand and share with other sinners both in and out of prison.

Mr. and Mrs. Roskolnikov will honeymoon in the nearest village, Yabakirsk, which, though nine thousand versts away from Moscow as the Imperial Eagle flies, offers such worthwhile tourist attractions as northern Siberia's preeminent theatrical group, the Yabakirsk Art Company, famous for its production of medieval morality plays. Mr. Roskolnikov is confident that, if his good conduct continues, the Imperial Ministry of Justice and Incarceration will permit them to depart on their honeymoon in Odessa in only seven more years.

TARZAN OF THE APES

JANE PARKER AND SIR JOHN GREYSTOKE

After a common-law relationship of six years, Jane Emily Parker, a daughter of Dr. and Mrs. Henry Parker of Hopkins Heights, Illinois, was formally married yesterday to Tarzan, as Sir John Greystoke, the son of the late Sir Cyril and the late Lady Cecilia Greystoke, is more commonly known to his tribal and animal friends in the jungles of Kenya and other countries in East Africa. The Reverend Dan Wright, an Australian missionary, performed the Methodist ceremony at the John Wesley Community House in Lower Tookba, a settlement about 125 miles southeast of Nairobi, the nearest town. Afterward, a second ceremony was performed by tribal elders from the region. The dusk-to-dawn drumming was performed by the ensemble of twenty-six warriors in traditional attire who had performed an even more elaborate ritual for the Prince and Princess of Wales while they were on an annual goodwill tour of Africa. Upon their return to London the Royal Couple made an emergency appointment at the Pelham Hearing Center on Harley Street.

The bride, 30, graduated from Oberlin College where she received a master's degree in soil conservation. Later, she received a grant from the Scoober Goober Peanut Butter Company to study soil conditions in East Africa. Her capture by cannibals, and eventual rescue by Tarzan, was featured in a recent issue of *The National Geographic* and will also be the subject of a forthcoming motion picture starring Gloria Swanson and George O'Brien.

The bridegroom, 36, bears the title of Lord of the Jungle, but, as a longtime disciple of George Bernard Shaw and the Fabian Society, he looks forward to a period in evolution when his animal friends are capable of understanding the principles of voting, so that they can choose their leader, hopefully a socialist, in a free election. He was lost in the jungle at the age of six when his parents, both prominent in the Royal Society for the Preservation of Colonial Wildlife, were ambushed and slain by the gang of ivory poachers whom they were pursuing. Reared by Cheetah, a chimpanzee, and Simba, a lion, he had no formal schooling, but was able to educate himself with the aid of the 21-volume *Oxford English Dictionary* and the 18-volume *Encyclopedia Britannica* that his late parents, devoted to *Times of London* crossword puzzles, always carried on their travels away from Surrey, to as near as Manchester and as far away as the South Pole. His recent book, *You Too Can Find Sex and True Happiness in the Jungle*, was so well received by readers in England and the United States that he is planning to lecture in those countries about the benefits of living close to nature and also wearing just a simple loincloth at all times except, of course, when invited to join the Royal Family for high tea at Buckingham Palace.

The ceremony was delayed for about twenty minutes, during which period the groom swung through the trees in search of Cheetah, his ring bearer, who had been enticed away from the clearing by a scent of ripe bananas.

PYGMALION/MY FAIR LADY

ELIZABETH DOOLITTLE AND HENRY HIGGINS

Elizabeth Victoria Doolittle, a daughter of Mr. and Mrs. Horatio Doolittle of Scavenger Alley in Whitechapel, was married yesterday in London to Henry Higgins, son of Mrs. Olivia Higgins and the late Albert Arthur George Higgins, Major General of the Queen's Royal Lancers. The Rev. Clyde Medford, who once studied diction with the groom at Demosthenes College in Edinburgh, performed the ceremony at St. Matthew's Church in Mayfair. His enunciation was flawless, and during the reception at the Dorchester Hotel in Park Lane, the groom suggested to his cousin, Philip Cunningham, the Archbishop of Canterbury, that the Rev. Medford was competent to participate in the forthcoming wedding of George Frederick Ernest Albert, the Prince of Wales, to Princess Mary of Teck at Westminster Abbey.

Known in her youth as Liza, Mrs. Higgins, 22, received her education in the alleys and back streets of Whitechapel, and majored in sibilants and dropped h's during her private studies with Mr. Higgins. She was, until her engagement to him, a retail outdoor florist near Covent Garden, where her father is a security expert and consultant to purveyors of fruits and vegetables when he is not offering his free adult education courses in current events and political philosophy in Hyde Park.

Mr. Higgins, 51, graduated from Cambridge University where he received a double doctorate in phonetics and philology and also the Samuel Johnson Gold Medal of the Royal Society for the Preservation and Improvement of English Diction. He was a fellow there for two years, until he and his colleague, Colonel Tobias Pickering, departed on a tour of the British Isles to record and catalogue the speech of their countrymen in all walks of life, even commoners like the current Mrs. Higgins. Toward the final phase of their tour, devoted to Huntington, Hartford and Hampshire, they were separated in a hurricane and did not meet again until twenty years later after a performance of, appropriately, *La Forza del Destino* outside Covent Garden. Colonel Pickering served as best man at the wedding, and was prepared not only with the traditional wedding ring but also with an atomizer should the bride and groom come down with hoarseness prior to the taking of their vows.

The bride wore a white silk wedding gown from the House of Worth in Paris. It was a gift from Her Majesty Queen Victoria, who has decreed that the bride's exquisite diction can only be due to her being a royal princess incognito, perhaps a granddaughter from the German, Greek, Russian, or Austro-Hungarian branch of her far-flung family.

THE PERRY MASON
DETECTIVE STORIES

DELLA STREET AND PERRY MASON

Della Jean Street, the daughter of Mr. and Mrs. Neil M. Street of Sacramento, was married yesterday in Washington, D.C., to Perry Mason, who was known by his given name, Percival Galahad Mason, until it was shortened by tabloid reporters during a case in which they referred to his client, Patricia Waring, as the Raunchy Redhead. The ceremony was performed in the John Marshall Room of the Mayflower Hotel by U.S. Supreme Court Chief Justice Warren Earl Burger, whom Mr. Mason used to tutor in the intricacies of jury selection when they were students together at St. Paul College of Law.

Mrs. Mason, 39, is the president, C.E.O. and chairwoman of Law Perfect, the school for legal secretaries that she established after resigning from the Los Angeles law firm headed by Mr. Mason, where she served as his private secretary for many years. She graduated magna cum laude from the Celestine

Gibbs School of Secretarial Arts and Sciences, where she was also the valedictorian of her class, her subject being secretarial skills as stepping stones to satisfactory spouses. Invited to remain at the school as a full professor, she was tempted to accept until she read in a law journal of an employment opportunity at the firm of Mr. Mason, who was currently defending Mrs. Tracy Rogers, called the Homicidal Honey by the media. Mrs. Mason was both National Typing Champion and National Shorthand Champion for seventeen years, until the competition was discontinued due to a lack of challengers.

Mr. Mason, 59, graduated magna cum laude from his postgraduate studies at Stanford Law School, after which he received a PhD in Courtroom Psychology at Harvard Law School. One of his classmates there was current Los Angeles District Attorney Hamilton Burger, who never won a case against Mr. Mason in the weekly mock trials.

Unless summoned to augment the defense team of slumlord Edward Graves, called by his tenants the Ravenous Realtor, Mr. and Mrs. Mason will be honeymooning at the Palm Beach estate of Mrs. Angela West, once a Burger King attendant. The tabloids had called her the Wayward Widow while Mr. Mason was defending her, with success, on a charge of having killed her billionaire husband, who suffered high cholesterol, with a daily breakfast, luncheon and dinner of a triple cheeseburger garnished with fries and onion rings.

THE THREE SISTERS

IRINA KROMENSKAYA AND
YEFREM ASOVITCH DENISON

TINA KROMENSKAYA AND
ANTON ANTONOVICH SITSKY

KATERINA KROMENSKAYA AND
SERGEI DMITRIVICH GOGSHOV

Irina Kromenskaya, Tina Kromenskaya, and Katerina Kromenskaya, the three daughters of the late Ilya Babovitch Kromenskay and the late Sonia Shostovoskiya of the isolated village of Bubinsk in the administrative district of Alexandervitch, were married yesterday, respectively, to Yefrem Asovitch Denisov, a son of Ivan Ivanovitch and Dasha Denisov of Klutskov in the Ukraine; to Anton Antonovitch Sitsky, a son of the Countess Elena Shiskova of St. Petersburg and the late Fyodor Igoritch Sitsky of Odessa; and to Sergei Dmitrivich Gogshov, son of Vladimir Ulmanov and Sofya Gogshova of Archangel.

Father Tikhon performed the ceremony that united the three sisters with their three grooms at the Cathedral of The Resurrection in Stumow. The choir, augmented with six additional bassos for the special occasion, was led by Choirmaster First Class Sergei Profomitch Mubitsky.

The father of the brides, until his death attributed to acute boredom, was a senior auxiliary real estate assessor first class in the province of Kimirsk, and his achievement in measuring the Great Grimov Swamp was recognized by His Highness Czar Nicholas with the Order of Boris, seventh degree. Their mother was for many years a marriage counselor to the Karenins, Oblonskys and other aristocratic families in the capital. She died within hours of partaking of a tainted sturgeon at a light refreshment after the funeral of Mrs. Karenina, who had ignored her famous precept, which says in its complete form, "All happy families are alike, and each unhappy family is unhappy in its own way, but they all need counseling for at least three sessions a week."

Mrs. Denisova, 34, graduated with honors from the Borodino Academy of Pedagogy. She taught the second grade at St. Vassili's School for twelve years, was bored every minute, and resigned within an hour after her engagement to Mr. Denisov.

Her bridegroom, 35, is a civil engineer third class at the Czarina Catherine the Great Waterworks in Kirkutsk. He is planning to write an analysis of the philosophy of Arthur Schopenhauer, and has already compiled three bushels of notes.

Mrs. Sitskya, 32, studied law at Boris Godounov University in Vtebst until she broke her pencil during a midterm examination and realized the futility of all her endeavors. She has since concentrated her energy upon the polishing of the family samovar and the preparing of tea and poppy seed cakes.

Mr. Sitsky, 39, who graduated from Prince Vassily College and holds a degree in peasant psychology, is a director fourteenth class of the Russian Express Company, and is in charge of their program to interest peasants in package tours to monasteries and other landmarks that will add to their patriotism and spiritual well-being.

Mrs. Gogshova, 27, studied the history of Utopias at the Prince Kropotkin Academy, but she was sick in bed with a cold on commencement day. Duke Gregor, the Czar's censor, closed the school the following day, and sentenced all its personnel, including the diploma distributor, to fifty years in Siberia. Mrs. Gogshova was never able to procure her diploma, nor a position of which she could be proud.

Mr. Gogshov, 28, studied pharmacology at Cantorsky College in Ibnist, and works at his family's pharmacy in Tzybukin. He plans to augment their current offerings to the public with the distribution of the *Russian National Enquirer*, a weekly illustrated magazine. Experts in the pharmaceutical business predict that magazines and migraine remedies will never mix.

The three sisters will honeymoon in Moscow starting on Sunday, a lucky day for travel, according to Anfisa, their old nurse. It has been their lifelong dream to visit that exciting and glorious city, so full of fine shops and theaters, and if their husbands are too busy to accompany them, as they rather expect, they will go themselves. If necessary, they will try to find comfort in the old Russian adage, "All women are daughters of Mother Eve, who was born to encounter serpents of all kinds." They do not expect to succeed in finding comfort in the adage.

THE ADVENTURES
OF SHERLOCK HOLMES

IRENE ADLER AND SHERLOCK HOLMES

I rene Adler, a woman of mystery who refuses
to reveal her family background, was married
yesterday to Sherlock Holmes, a consulting
detective. Officiating jointly at the ceremony in the
Forest of Arden Room of the Savoy Hotel were Rabbi
Jonas Cohen of the Kensington Green Synagogue and
the Reverend Arthur Templeton of the Church of the
Redeemer in the Strand, where the groom had once
foiled the theft of a world-famous rose window during
a requiem mass for the Duke of Burlington. About
a half hour before the wedding ceremony, when the
bride noticed that all the flowers were missing, the
groom leaped into a hansom and recovered them at
the home of his archenemy and the most dangerous
man in all England, Professor James Moriarty.

Beyond the fact that she once blackmailed her
kindergarten teacher at a public school for gifted,
charming, but sociopathic children in Trenton, New

Jersey, little is known of the formal education of Mrs. Holmes. It has been rumored that she was responsible for the monstrous crime at the Westminster Bank on Threadneedle Street in June of last year. Disguised as Her Majesty Queen Victoria, and escorted by a troop of cavalry in full regalia, a woman drove up to the bank in what appeared to be the royal coach, and once inside the premises, she demanded that they immediately cash her personal check for a million guineas.

Mr. Holmes, 42, is the son of Giles and Julia Holmes, the proprietors of Hillcrest House, a hotel for respectable ladies and gentlemen in Brighton. When all too many of the respectable ladies and gentlemen began to "skip out" before paying for their accommodations, Mr. Holmes, then in his first year at Eton, decided to put his unique powers of deduction to good effect, and he succeeded in apprehending all the defalcators. For the last twelve years he has practiced his unique profession in his upstairs flat at 221-B Baker Street, and he will continue to live there with his friend and associate, Dr. John Watson, while Mrs. Holmes travels abroad in search of business opportunities.

The ceremony was interrupted briefly by Chief Inspector Douglas L. Lestrade of Scotland Yard, who wished to consult the groom about the strange disappearance of five Indian elephants from the

London zoo. Thanks to the advice of the groom, Chief Inspector Lestrade was able to find them within the hour at a display of Mrs. Bing's old-fashioned peanut brittle at Harrod's food court.

HOMER'S ODYSSEY

PENELOPE AND ODYSSEUS

Adhering to the ancient tradition which decrees a renewal of vows between a husband and wife who have been apart for longer than an ennaeteris, or nine lunar years, Queen Penelope, the daughter of King Icarius and Queen Periboea of Sparta, was remarried yesterday morning to King Odysseus of Ithaca, the son of retired King Laertes and the late Queen Anticlea. With the direct inspiration of Zeus, Athena and all the other deities, and after the prescribed sacrifices and libations to them and to his ancestors, King Laertes performed the ceremony in the family chamber at the palace in Ithaca. The chamber and all of the palace were still fragrant from the sacramental oils with which King Odysseus, assisted by his son, Prince Telemachus, had purified them after his well-justified slaughter of insolent Antinous and the ninety-nine other suitors who had harassed Penelope while he fulfilled his state duties and participated in the expedition to rescue Queen Helen from the Trojans.

King Odysseus paid King Icarius a bride-price of seventy-two oxen, forty horses, twelve gold goblets, and an assortment of spears and swords. In keeping with ancient tradition, King Icarius presented the same number of animals, vessels, and weaponry to the bride. King Icarius also paid Chidius of Thasos two golden goblets for his composition of the bridal song, which was performed with dancing by an augmented troupe from Arcadia. The banquet included rare meads and wines from throughout the Mediterranean, and the wild boars were personally slaughtered and trimmed by Eumaeus the royal swineherd, who had remained faithful to the groom during his absence of twenty years. The table scraps were enjoyed by Argus, the king's old and loyal dog, who had recognized him when he returned to Ithaca in the guise of a beggar.

The bride, 38, studied spinning and weaving with Aristoxenus of Sardes, who, according to legend, learned the crafts from Athena and Hera. Shrouds are her specialty, and they are reputed to be a special comfort to wearers in their journey across the River Styx.

The groom, 45, was trained in the arts of war and government by his father, King Laertes, and his grandfather, King Autolycus. His skills were well displayed during the siege of Troy, where he coordinated the activity of such brave but egotistic warriors as Achilles and Agamemnon. Later, he commanded the heroes who hid in the wooden horse and then leaped out and conquered Troy.

King Scyllis of Boeotia has offered the newlyweds the use of his summer palace for their honeymoon, but the groom declined with thanks. He added that after his having traversed the wine-dark seas for twenty years, only the gods can ever make him stir from his family and island kingdom.

MARY POPPINS

MARY POPPINS AND BERT CAPER

Mary Elizabeth Victoria Poppins, the very efficient daughter of Mr. and Mrs. Nicholas Poppins of Chatham Green, was married yesterday to Herbert Albert Caper, the son of Thomas and Alice Caper of South Hornchurch. The Rev. Edward Wipple performed the ceremony at St. Brigit's Church in Chelsea.

Mrs. Caper, forever 29, graduated with all 23 annual awards from the Spick-and-Span Institute in Greenwich and then majored in advanced discipline at Mrs. Campbell's College for Governesses and Nannies. In her first position, at a noble but rowdy residence in Berkeley Square, she was so adept at teaching good manners to her three young charges that, during breakfast, they even stopped throwing their kipper bones at the servants. Although Mrs. Caper herself would never accept a shilling that she had not earned by the sweat of her brow, her ability to communicate with horses and other animals has resulted in many a profitable wager at the Derby for her employers.

Mr. Caper, 36, was suspended permanently from the Camden Town Grammar School on his first day in kindergarten, when his teacher caught him admiring a rather risqué photo of Toots Cooper, a music hall performer. He learned art by studying the graffiti on the posters he passed on his way to the Goose and Swan, the pub where he daily fetched their pints of Guinness for his Mum and Pa. His sidewalk drawings outside the National Gallery have been admired by French landscape painter Claude Monet, among other artists and connoisseurs. He once tried to paint on canvas in an indoor studio, but was discouraged when the hours went by and he didn't hear a single coin drop into his outstretched cap on the floor.

Because of previous commitments in India and Burma, King Edward and Queen Alexandra were unable to attend the ceremony, but as a token of their eternal gratitude to the bride for her occasional emergency services in the royal nursery at Windsor Castle, they lent the services of Sir Christopher Fugue, who performed his fourteen variations on the bride's favorite nursery song, "All Things Bright and Dutiful."

LA BOHEME and LA TRAVIATA

MIMI COLOMBO AND RODOLFO FONTANA

VIOLETTA VALERY AND ALFREDO GERMONT

Mimi Colombo, a daughter of Susanne and Marcello Colombo, both deceased, was married on Sunday to Rodolfo Fontana, a son of Caramia and Giovanni Fontana, also both deceased. At the same time, in a double wedding, Violetta Valery, a daughter of Gina and Antonio Valery, was married to Alfredo Germont, the son of Alberto and the late Elena Germont. Father Giulio Montemezzi, the recent confessor of both brides, performed the ceremony in the Church of Our Blessed Savior, which serves the faithful who, like the two brides, require occasional treatment for pulmonary afflictions at the Fiorentino Sanitarium, located near the village of Ferrarese in the Italian Alps.

Mrs. Fontana, 20, was an embroiderer of flowers until she succumbed to consumption in her unheated room in the Latin Quarter of Paris and required prolonged but eventually successful treatment at the sanitarium. One of her ancestors, Francesca Colombo, is credited with the original recipe for french-fried potatoes in 1677. Until they died of malnutrition and overwork, her parents were laborers on a beet and turnip farm in Normandy.

Mr. Fontana, 26, studied painting in the atelier of Pepe Brabantio in Montmartre. When he could no longer pay for his tuition and models, he decided to paint only landscapes, and eventually perfected a style that he called Pre-Impressionism. Thanks to an article in *The Beaux Arts Courier* by two of his disciples, Claude Monet and Camille Pisarro, his complete stock of canvases, with a single exception, was sold to J. C. Nickel, the American millionaire and connoisseur, for eventual contribution to the Metropolitan Museum of Art in New York City. The painting withheld from sale was a portrait of the artist's bride, which will hang in the parlor of their home in Provence. Because Mrs. Fontana is susceptible to chills, every room will have a fireplace and western exposure.

Mrs. Germont, 32, dropped out of the St. Genevieve Academy in Rambouillet, where she was bored with her classmates and the quality and quantity of the local wines, truffles and croissants. After fleeing to Paris, she became a popular hostess and a nocturnal companion of a succession of rich and dissolute men, including Baron Douphol.

Mr. Germont, 32, is administrator of his family's estate in Provence. He graduated from the Charpentier College of Agriculture, where he wrote a treatise on the rotation of crops. His article on the benefits of romaine lettuce with French dressing, which appeared in a recent issue of the *Toulouse Journal of Agriculture*, was acclaimed by the National Association of Salad Chefs.

Just in time for Sunday's ceremony, Mr. Germont was able to cultivate and arrange a wedding bouquet of camellias, the favorite flower of his bride. Not to be outdone by the devotion of his friend at the altar, Mr. Colombo painted a picture of his bride in her wedding gown, for which she had personally embroidered the flowers. She will retire from her profession after honoring a commitment to embroider a wedding gown for her friend Mitzi Carrière, who is hoping against hope to receive a proposal of marriage from at least one of her many lovers, which include famed author Guy de Maupassant.

Though Mrs. Germont is almost completely cured of consumption and hypotension, her overindulgence in champagne is still an occasional problem, and she and her groom, combining therapy and pleasure, will honeymoon in a cottage on the grounds of Overindulgers Anonymous near Montmercy.

NURSERY RHYMES FROM MOTHER GOOSE

THE OLD WOMAN WHO LIVED IN A SHOE
AND OLD KING COLE

Rebecca Adidas, the daughter of the late Mr. and Mrs. Antonio Gucci of Milan, was married yesterday to His Royal Highness, King Cole of Nursery Rhyme Land. Father Short conducted the service at The Little Church Down the Lane. The wedding march was played by the King's personal ensemble, The Fiddlers Three, and the traditional wedding songs were sung by Little Tommy Tucker. Being a loyal subject, Mr. Tucker refused to accept his usual fee of five pieces of silver, and said that his supper would be sufficient remuneration.

The bride, 75, is the widow of the late Hans Adidas, and the mother of eight girls and twelve boys, all with hearty appetites. In his will, Mr. Adidas bequeathed to her his ancestral residence, which was a shoe, but he left her with so little money that when her children would clamor for one of the pies extolled by their playmate Simple Simon, she would usually beat them all soundly and put them to bed.

King Cole, 83, graduated from Heidelberg University where he majored in political science and public administration. Ever since his coronation after the death of his father King Dole, still revered by his subjects for the unemployment benefit named for him, King Cole has devoted himself so completely to affairs of state and the welfare of his subjects that he could never find the time to marry and provide an heir to his throne. Since becoming an octogenarian, he has been especially interested in the problems of the elderly, and when Mother Goose, his Minister of Geriatric Welfare, informed him of the many problems of the Old Woman Who Lived in a Shoe and lacked even a shoe horn for the convenience of corpulent guests, he decided that it was a matter to which he must attend personally, and at once.

One of the incidental joys of matrimony for King Cole is that, after his adoption of his bride's children, he now has twenty heirs and heiresses for his throne. One of the detriments is that Her Highness, Queen Rebecca, disapproves of his smoking his pipe in the royal palace, and she has designated her former residence, the shoe, as the royal smoking area.

IN SEARCH OF LOST TIME

GILBERTE SWANN AND MARCEL X

Gilberte Swann, the daughter of Mr. Charles Swann and Mrs. Odette de Crécy Swann of Combray and Paris, was married yesterday to Marcel X, the son of Mr. Paul and Mrs. Paulette X, also of Combray and Paris, but residing in a less exclusive arrondissement than the Swanns. After an epithalamium by Guy Venteuil of the Paris Opera, recently admired for his Mephistopheles in Gounod's *Faust*, Bishop Jean Le Tour, elevated last Easter by the Pope, performed the ceremony at the season's most fashionable church in Paris, St. Emilie's in the Faubourg Saint-Germaine.

The bride's father, acclaimed on all the boulevards as the Prince of Dandies until the retirement of his favorite tailor on the Rue du Faubourg Saint-Martin, is a member of both the Jockey Club and the Legion of Honor. Her mother, until her marriage, was, as they say, an interior decorator, and her unique services were in constant demand in some of the most exclusive and aristocratic bedrooms in Paris. The groom's parents are a more retiring couple, and Mrs. X is never happier than when she and Françoise, her servant, are baking a batch of madeleines for Marcel and bourgeois friends and guests.

Mrs. X, 18, learned her catechism and secular studies at St. Ursula's School for Young Ladies from Better Families. She considered studying the history of French poetry at the Sorbonne until her mother warned her that she might meet there both teachers and students who were below her station in life and who also approved of free verse, a slippery slope to Free Thought and free schooling for the hoi polloi. She and Marcel were childhood acquaintances during their summer vacations in Combray, and after a long separation devoted mostly to rolling hoops and emotional self-examination, they met again one day in a park on the Champs Elysèes.

Mr. X, 20, is a student of everything under the sun, both in France and in countries that can accommodate his high standard of living. He still seeks his life's vocation, and toward that end has cultivated an acquaintance with people in all walks of French life, especially such aristocrats as Mme. de Villeparis, a connection of the Duke and Duchess de Guermantes, and her nephews Robert de Saint-Loup and the

Baron de Charlus. Occasionally, while sipping tisane or nibbling a madeleine, he trembles on the brink of a great discovery about life, art and time, and about France and the future disposition of its social classes and their sexual preferences.

Unless they are invited at the last minute in the immediate future to a reception at Buckingham Palace in London, the newlyweds will honeymoon in Venice, where the groom has come to believe that, during or immediately after the consumption of a madeleine, the swaying of the gondolas at twilight are capable of revealing life's ultimate secrets to a sensitive Frenchman like himself.

THE WIZARD OF OZ

GLINDA, THE GOOD FAIRY, AND
JASON, THE WIZARD OF OZ

Glinda, the Good Fairy, a daughter of Priscilla, the Good Witch of the Southeast, and of Arthur, the Good Warlock of the Northeast, was married yesterday to Jason, the Wizard of Oz, a son of Damon and Genevieve, the Wizard and Sorceress of Unz. Justice Dan Sanders performed the ceremony in the sun parlor of the Baker farm about a dozen miles north of Jackson Gulch, Kansas.

Earlier in the day, upon being awakened by her dog Toto, Dorothy Baker, the young niece of Ed and Em Baker, owners of the farm, looked through her bedroom window and observed from the weather vane in the corn field that a cyclone was heading for the area. She wanted to phone the bride and groom and suggest that they postpone the wedding, but upon the advice of three more positive-thinking friends—the Cowardly Lion, the Tin Man and the Scarecrow—she phoned instead the parents of the bride and groom and suggested that they use their skills and good offices to provide good weather and possibly even a rainbow for the ceremony.

The bride graduated from the Fairyland Institute of Arts and Sciences, where she majored in Orthomalevistry, the overcoming of the spells and other evil machinations of bad witches, in particular those of the Wicked Witch of the West. She refused to speculate whether the cyclone indicated on Dorothy's weather vane had been instigated by the Wicked Witch of the West or other present or former antagonists in her battle to assist young women such as Dorothy to find their way home after being lost in a strange place and without access to either public or private transportation. Last year she won a golden wand from the Faith and Family Foundation of Oz for her prize-winning composition on how to improve family values in twenty-five words or less: "Close your eyes and tap your heels together three times. And think to yourself, there's no place like home."

The groom received his master's degree in necromancy from the Merlin Academy near Stonehenge in England. In addition to heading the Department of Social Welfare and Supernatural Services in Oz, he is a regular consultant to the Kansas City District Bank of the U.S. Federal Reserve System and to J. P. Morgan and Associates, the Wall Street investment bankers.

In honor of the occasion, the groom's parents arranged for the Munchkin Construction Co. to build a yellow brick road across the two miles of swampland from State Highway 201 to the Baker farm. After the departure of their guests, the newlyweds set out along the bright new road for their secret honeymoon retreat that was somewhere over the rainbow.

THE SUN ALSO RISES

LADY BRETT ASHLEY AND JAKE BARNES

In a sunrise ceremony at The Lost and Found Generation Church on the Left Bank in Paris, Lady Brett Madeline Ashley, the daughter of Lord Robert and Lady Cynthia Burlington of Hyde Manor in Somersetshire, was married yesterday to John Scott Barnes, a son of Mrs. Gladys Barnes of Chicago and Dr. Victor Barnes of Dallas. The groom's parents, who had not seen each other since their divorce twenty years ago, commended their son for his bravery at the altar, and offered him the names of their lawyers, just in case. The Rev. Charles Penniell officiated, after which he rushed off to Provence for the trout fishing and then to Rome for the pollo alla zingara at the Hostaria dell'Orso. Henry Rolles, who played a medley of wedding marches on the organ, rushed off to Pamplona for the bullfights and then to Heidelberg for a wine-tasting party that, hopefully but not inevitably, would include that fabulous vintage, Mussbacher Eselshaut Auslese 1919.

Mrs. Barnes, 35 and proud of each tumultuous year, attended Somerville Hall College at Oxford until, after an emergency meeting of the Board of Governors, her nightly parties were declared detrimental to the morals and scholarship of the entire university. When her first husband, Captain Raymond Ashley, was killed in the Battle of Verdun, she wrote a nasty letter to Kaiser Wilhelm, and then fell into a chronic depression from which she sought relief in rare cognac, four-star cuisine, travel, fashion shows, and liaisons with whatever wealthy men were available at the time and place. Of the men she met, she was deeply attracted only to Jake Barnes, even though his war wounds would prevent the physical activities that women expect in a marriage.

Mr. Barnes, 38, majored in journalism at Yale University until he terminated his studies because he had come to believe that he was not learning the real truth about life, and about men and women, and about how to report their activities even though these activities were, in the long run, as senseless as the coming and going of ants and bees. Two years ago, after a last taxi drive in Madrid with the then Lady Ashley, his love for her, combined with his sexual inadequacy, caused him to attempt suicide by entering an enclosure occupied by El Malicioso, a particularly vicious bull that had already gored twelve picadors and six matadors. Fortunately for his relationship with Lady Ashley and their later mutual satisfaction as husband and wife, he was spotted in time by the bull's personal veterinarian, Dr. Fernando Lopez, a urologist who specialized in multi-species male potency and restorative surgery at the University of Toledo.

The newlyweds will honeymoon at the four-star Hotel de Madame DuBarry in Périgord. They were bored out of their skulls on a previous visit, and this time expect to be eventually bored also with lovemaking, but they hope once again to find solace in the scallops with black truffles at Chez Hermione's, located at 21 Rue de la Mairie in nearby Dordogne. They despair of ever finding again the cool pear cider, reminiscent of Provence, that was once offered them in a dim bistro in Montmartre, on a narrow street that was later devastated and then modernized to include a McPierre's, the fast-food chain that offers greasy sausages on a bun and four varieties of fermented goat's milk.

THE ADVENTURES OF DON QUIXOTE

THE FAIR DULCINEA AND
DON QUIXOTE DE LA MANCHA

Dulcinea del Toboso, the virtuous and beautiful, graceful and accomplished daughter of Alfredo and Maria Lorenzo, realized the ultimate felicity of her sex when she was married yesterday to the most valiant knight who ever lived in all Spain if not in all Christendom, His Excellency Nonpareil Don Quixote de la Mancha. Cardinal Miguel del Alvarado y Primavera, primate of Iberia and the Pope's own confessor should he ever have a sin to confess, performed the ceremony at the Church of Santa Lucia in Seville. The bride's father, who can trace his ancestry to Isaac of Gilladado, a first cousin of St. Paul, neé Saul of Tarsus, owns a small estate whose vineyards produce the wines and brandies preferred by royal gourmets.

Doña Dulcinea graduated magna cum laude from the Convent of the Immaculate Conception in Toledo, where her unique vocal skills permitted her to sing both as a soprano and contralto in the choir. During the winter months, she always donated the firewood for her cell to the poor of the parish, and when she invariably came down with a cold, she always donated her cough medicines to the sick. In a pre-marriage ritual that her family has practiced for more than five hundred years, ever since the glorious days of Count Fernán González of Burgos, the bride's duenna, Doña Juanita Guitarrez, swore upon the Holy Bible that her charge was as virginal as she was virtuous. Doña Dulcinea is a patron of the Queen Isabella School for Orphans, which teaches flamenco dancing and other practical skills.

The bridegroom is a direct descendent of Ruy Díaz de Bivar, also known as El Cid, who conquered Valencia in 1094 and halted the Moorish expansion in Spain. He studied fencing and the other martial arts while serving as a squire with his uncle, Count Juan Hernando de Castro. He was personally knighted by His Royal Highness King Philip III after he single-handedly wiped out a troop of English invaders who were on a mission to destroy all the churches, monasteries and nunneries in the kingdom. On a later campaign in behalf of God and country, he foiled the invasion of a gang of giants who, employing a new French technique called camouflage, had disguised themselves as windmills.

The newlyweds will honeymoon in Gibraltar, where Don Quixote hopes to combine the business of knight gallantry with the pleasure of marriage by repelling an invasion by the English, which he believes is imminent. Sancho Panza, the don's squire, who is famed for his realism, believes that never in a million years will the English ever dare to invade a Spanish stronghold like Gibraltar.

OUR TOWN

THE LATE EMILY WEBB GIBBS AND THE LATE GEORGE GIBBS

The late Emily Webb Gibbs and the late George Gibbs were remarried yesterday afternoon in an informal and private ceremony at the First Congregational Church in Grover's Corner, New Hampshire. It is the very site where they were originally married, forty-seven years ago in earth time, at the height of the baseball season.

In 1913, Emily died in childbirth at the age of 25. She was the mother of Robert Emile Gibbs, now 47, who has inherited her blue eyes and the bright smile that, as the old saying goes, could charm a robin from a tree. George died yesterday morning at the age of 72. He and Robert had been devoted to the growing of organic apples, cherries and other fruits on the farm that has been in the Gibbs family since 1830, the year that Sarah J. Hale, a distant relative, wrote the immortal poem beloved by children the world over, "Mary Had a Little Lamb." Their grandchildren, Emily and Roger, and their spouses, Henry and Lucy, were in charge of processing and marketing the cider, vinegar and maple syrup. All the farm's products have been frequent winners in their category at the state fair in Concord, and their jams and apple butters have been top-rated by *Consumer Reports* and have won the coveted seal of approval of *Good Housekeeping* magazine.

George was the oldest active member of the Grover's Corner Voluntary Fire Department, and after a severe case of smoke inhalation suffered on Tuesday during a fire at the Josiah and Marcy Jenkins Free Library and Auditorium on Pierce Street, he died peacefully in his sleep yesterday in Washington Community Hospital. His son, grandchildren, and the spirit of Emily, his wife, were at his bedside.

Because their first marriage had been such a "swell experience," George and Emily decided to renew their vows at the First Congregational Church, still at the corner of Cannon Street and Scammel Lane, and still in need of a new piano or at least a tuning, and then they ascended to heaven together. On their way, they detoured over to the baseball field in Webster Park, and were pleased to observe that George's old team, the Grover's Corner Grizzlies, were beating the heck out of their old rivals, the Lake Washington Wolverines.

THE NANCY DREW MYSTERY STORIES

NANCY DREW AND NED NICKERSON

Police Captain Nancy Drew, the daughter of Carson and the late Deborah Drew of River Heights, was married in that town yesterday to Edward Francis Nickerson, son of Warren and Louise Nickerson of Mapleton. The Rev. Ben Miller officiated at the ceremony at the Clark St. Baptist Church, where the bride and groom once combined their skills in detection and, after their discovery of only a single clue, a peacock's feather in a rear pew, they were able to recover the poor box that had been stolen by the notorious Mr. Swifty Morgan after services on Christmas Day.

The organ selections at the wedding, attended by Police Chief Cal McGinnis and many of the grateful people they had assisted over the years in cases with such obscure clues as broken lockets and velvet masks, were performed by Emily Bennett, whose priceless instrument, the largest organ in Mapleton, was also once stolen, and then later recovered in London's St.

Paul's Cathedral by the bride and groom while they were still amateur detectives.

Captain Drew, 28, who is retaining her maiden name for professional as well as feminist reasons, majored in criminology at Harper University, where she graduated summa cum laude. She later graduated from the Milwaukee Police Academy and became the first police captain of her sex in the history of that city. On her very first assignment, her discovery of an elephant's tusk in a booth in a Howard Johnson's restaurant led to the capture of Nicholas "Killer Nick" James, who had been eluding authorities for almost a decade.

Mr. Nickerson, 31, who still prefers to be called Ned rather than Edward, heads the Milwaukee office of Crime Busters, the internationally famous detective agency. He graduated from Emerson Police College, where he majored in kidnapping, both of humans and animals. His recovery of Rufus, the Seeing Eye dog abducted by a gang headed by crime boss Robert "Blind Bob" Dollmann, was the subject of a recent article in *The Saturday Evening Post*.

The bride wore a white satin gown with full train that had been worn previously by her maternal grandmother, Mrs. Irma Elkins, former proprietor of the Windsor Theater in Sage City. In the summer of

1944, Mrs. Elkins's festival of Shirley Temple films, accompanied by free lollipops, was acclaimed by Gov. Marvin Hudson as a unique cultural contribution to Sage City if not to all Sage County.

Just before the benediction by the Rev. Miller, when the bride spotted a looting in progress of the poor box located in the rear of the church, she pulled off her gown, adjusted her blue uniform with matching silver buttons and silver bars, pulled out her service revolver, leaped from the chancel, and ran down the nave to apprehend the felon. He turned out to be her old foe, Swifty Morgan, who had been recently released from prison. Before being led away by Chief McGinness, Mr. Morgan requested to kiss the bride. She acceded, after he promised on her bridal Bible to go straight when he next emerged from prison.

WASHINGTON SQUARE/THE HEIRESS

CATHERINE SLOPER AND MORRIS TOWNSEND

Catherine Sloper, the daughter and heiress of the late Dr. Austin Sloper and the late Geraldine Sloper of New York City, is to be married today to Morris Townsend, the son of Kenneth and Marie Townsend of El Dorado, California, at the bride's home at 20 Washington Square North.

The daughter of one of the reigning beauties of her generation, Miss Sloper, 32, is admired by discerning New Yorkers for her gentle disposition and expertise at petit point. She acquired the latter accomplishment from her Aunt Henrietta Pennyman of Poughkeepsie, widow of the late Reverend E. Jason Pennyman, whose sermons, almost a year after his death, are still quoted as far away as Newburgh and Albany.

Miss Sloper's engagement was once in abeyance, due to her father's belief that she lacked beauty and charm and that Mr. Townsend's sole interest in her was her future inheritance from him. Dr. Sloper's health, hitherto robust, went into a sudden and mysterious decline in recent weeks. According to Dr. Edward Blythe, Dr. Sloper's longtime colleague at Beekman Hospital, the cause of death was a combination of overwork and a psychosomatic reaction to his daughter's stubborn resistance to his plans for her.

Mr. Townsend, 33, received a master's degree in engineering from Harvard University. He is the benefactor of many charities in California, and recently contributed an organ to St. Paul's Episcopal Church in San Francisco. Since the retirement of his father, he has been the president and chief executive officer of the Eureka Gold Mining Company, established in 1848 and already one of the most profitable businesses in the country. Because of his great wealth, he long feared that young women and their parents would be more interested in his fortune than in his personal qualities, and so it had become his practice, when away from California, to present himself as being without financial prospects or even a respectable profession.

In addition to possessing a quiet charm and the sort of reticent beauty that is often overlooked in bustling cities like New York, Miss Sloper was the first young woman to ever appreciate Mr. Townsend for his modesty and character, and was willing to risk her financial security and accept the hand of a pauper. He forgives her father for opposing their union so strenuously, and will, upon returning from their honeymoon in Europe, establish in his memory a Dr. Austin Sloper Free Clinic in several of the slum districts of New York City.

Officiating at the private ceremony will be the Reverend James Lispenard of the Duane Street Methodist Church, to which the bride and groom had once planned to elope until their plans were foiled by the misguided machinations of the late Dr. Sloper. "All's well that weds well," says the Reverend Lispenard, who is famed throughout Lower Manhattan for his wit as well as piety.

THE HUNCHBACK OF NOTRE DAME

ESMERALDA SPINADA AND QUASIMODO GUISOT

Esmeralda Spinada, a daughter of Fortunato and Esperanza Spinada, who claim to be the king and queen of French gypsies, was married yesterday to Quasimodo Guisot, of unknown parentage. However, the straw basket in which the groom was found, upon the steps of an orphanage in Montmartre, has been identified by an officer of the Ancient and Loyal Guild of Weavers as having been made in northeast Provence. Father Ignatius Amadeus Musset officiated in the subterranean chapel reserved for peasants and other commoners at the Cathedral of Notre Dame in Paris, where the groom has long been the official bell ringer.

Mrs. Guisot, 27, graduated from the Romany College of the Performing Arts, where she received degrees in folk dancing and composition. She is a member of the All-Girl Tambourine Quartet, which performs nightly on the sidewalks of Paris until residents summon the gendarmes. Often accused of the theft of purses and jewelry, she has yet to be caught in the act by her alleged victims.

Mr. Guisot, 34, graduated with honors from the Notre Dame School of Bell Ringing, where he received his doctorate in vespers and Easter masses. He is now on the faculty of that institution. Being a hunchback since birth, he has devoted his life, in addition to Notre Dame and bell ringing, to helping compatriots with his own and related handicaps, and he was the founder of the Pièta Society, a social service organization that rehabilitates victims of spinal and skeletal disorders. Its work in dungeons throughout the kingdom has been commended by both King Louis and the Count de Bergerac, the royal torturer.

During their honeymoon in Italy, the groom will combine business with pleasure and conduct a master's class in advanced bell ringing at St. Peter's Basilica in Rome.

THE IMPORTANCE OF BEING EARNEST

ROSEMARY PRISM AND THE REV. MAXIMILIAN CHASUBLE

osemary Mabel Prism, the daughter of Mr.
and Mrs. Clive Prism of Dinworthy in Devon,
was married yesterday afternoon to the Rev.
Canon Maximilian Albert Chasuble, the son of
Claude Chasuble of Wallingford in Berkshire and of
the late Marianne Chasuble. The Right Reverend J.
Northcombe Wittaker, bishop of Shropshire, officiated
at the wedding in the garden at the Manor House in
Woolton, Shropshire. The garden was recently the
site of two other weddings, that of the bride's former
employer, Mr. Ernest John Moncrieff, to the Hon.
Gwendolen Fairfax, and of Mr. Algernon Moncrieff to
Miss Cecily Cardew, a former ward of Mr. Ernest John
Moncrieff and a former pupil of the bride.

Mrs. Chasuble graduated from the Imperial Night
School of Nursemaids and Nannies in Greenwich.
After the misplacement of a succession of infants

and toddlers at Victoria Station and other locales throughout the British Isles, she enrolled for additional studies at Mrs. Burney's Academy of Governesses and Paid Companions. Her sad experiences with youngsters prompted her parents to leave domestic service and to establish the Prism Agency, which searches for lost children, both in and away from Victoria Station.

The Rev. Chasuble graduated from St. Saviour's Grammar School in Bermondsey and then, summa cum laude, from the True Cross Divinity School at Tuddenham in Suffolk. He is the canon of St. Christopher's Cathedral in Wanstead in Shropshire. He has written extensively about church rites and rituals, especially christenings, and his book of memoirs, *From Badminton Court to Baptistery Font*, has been a modest but perennial favorite at Foyle's Bookshop in London and as far away as Brentano's Bookshop in New York City. In a forthcoming work, *The Importance of Being Christened*, he will argue that being properly christened by an ordained minister of the Church of England is far more important than, for example, the recent desire of his wife's former employer for being named Ernest.

Their honeymoon trip to Brighton was delayed for six hours; Mrs. Chasuble had misplaced her husband in the waiting room of the railroad station in Woolton.

THE MERCHANT OF VENICE

PORTIA AND SHYLOCK

Portia, a daughter of the late Ferencio and Viveria, was married last night in Venice to Shylock, son of the late Benjamino and Rachela. Rabbi Jacobo ben Davido performed the ceremony at Beth Israel Synagogue in the Jewish quarter called the Ghetto.

Mrs. Shylock, 34, is the widow of the late Bassanio, a famous man-about-town and friend of Antonio, a local merchant. Mrs. Shylock is famous throughout Venice and northern Italy for her eloquence, which once saved the life of Antonio in a famous legal dispute over the extraction of a pound of flesh. But it is this same vocal talent that had marred her marriage to Bassanio, who preferred peace and quiet in their modest palace on the Grand Canal after he returned home after a day and evening of gambling, drinking and carousing with his friends Antonio, Solanio, Salarino, and Gratiano. Bassanio died unexpectedly last year at the Casa Lolita, a pleasure establishment on the Rialto. Antonio, his companion that night, explained to all who would listen that they had gone there, on a self-appointed mission of civic pride, to persuade the proprietor and his clients and personnel to join them in their restoration of Venetian landmarks before the start of the tourist season,

Mr. Shylock, 59, is a retired personal banker, and though he had suffered in more ways than financially after his dealings with Portia and her friends, he had been so impressed by her eloquence regarding the universality of human suffering that, upon hearing of the death of Bassanio, he sent her both a note of condolence and a memorial wreath from the garden of Beth Israel Synagogue, which he has served, without remuneration, as sexton and financial consultant since his retirement from banking.

Upon receipt of the note and flowers, Mrs. Shylock was so deeply moved by this display of fellow feeling that, through her servant Balthazar, she arranged for a meeting with her former foe at Nathanio's, a kosher café in King Solomon Square in the Ghetto. By the afternoon of the meeting, she had studied the elements of Judaism and come to realize that it was the mother religion of her own, and that she could never hope to be a good Christian until she converted to Judaism.

After the formal conclusion of the marriage ceremony with a benediction by Rabbi Jacobo, Mrs. Shylock proceeded to offer an impromptu discourse, in ancient Hebrew, on the conduct and virtues of Jewish wives, and whether a challah, the traditional Sabbath bread, should have raisins all the year round or only on certain Holy Days. At the advice of his daughter Jessica, with whom he was on the best of terms again, Shylock dispatched a servant to Nathanio's with the message that the wedding feast would not begin till midnight or thereabouts.

PETER PAN

WENDY DARLING AND SIR PETER PAN ADAIR

Wendy Angela Darling, the daughter of Mr. and Mrs. Michael Darling of West Kensington in London, was married yesterday to Sir Peter Pan Adair, C.B., the son of Sir John and Lady Amelia Adair of St. John's Wood, also in London. The Right Rev. J. Algernon Holdridge performed the ceremony at the Church of St. Martin's in the Fields. Sir Otto Fleming played at the organ until he was chased from the loft by a ferocious intruder with a hooked arm and wearing a pirate costume. The reception was held at the Oberon Room of the Savoy Hotel on the Strand.

Lady Wendy, 26, attended Lady Bedelia Portland's Academy for Young Ladies in Tavistock Square. There she made the honors list for hoop rolling, and her record time for the Embankment foot race from Waterloo Bridge to Blackfriar's Bridge has never been approached. In honor of her triumph in hoop-rolling at the 1896 Olympic games in Athens, Queen Victoria commissioned Sir Edward Elgar to compose a march entitled "Pomp and Circumference."

Sir Peter, 27, was enrolled at the Cobbett Boys' School in Bloomsbury until he relocated to Never-Never Land, where his principal interest was juvenology, the prolongation of the juvenile personality and its interests and activities. Among the skills he cultivated and perfected there was flying, both unassisted and mechanical. Eventually, with the cooling of relations between Britain and Germany, he heeded the advice of his friends Tiger Lily and Tinker Belle, and he returned to England to offer his services to his Sovereign and to his country. He is currently a test pilot for the Royal Air Force and also the Regius Professor of Aerodynamics at Trinity College in Cambridge. Upon the order of the Sovereign, and then a standing ovation in the House of Lords, he became a Companion of the Bath last spring.

Before the couple could depart on their honeymoon on the Isle of Wight, Sir Peter received a most urgent message from 10 Downing Street. In response, and without the assistance of a mechanical gadget, Sir Peter flew through the worst London fog and Channel storm in decades to the Elysee Palace in Paris, there to deliver the hamper of fish and chips that the Prime Minister had left behind in his haste to cement relations with France before President Emile Loubet could sign a treaty with Kaiser Wilhelm of Germany.

THE GREAT GATSBY

DAISY BUCHANAN AND JAY GATSBY

Daisy Buchanan, the daughter of Mr. and Mrs. Walter Hartsdale of Nouveau Riche, Michigan, was married yesterday to Jason Schuyler Gatsby, a son of Mr. and Mrs. Melvin Gatz of Shady Side, Indiana. The groom's parents could not attend, due to previous commitments to the Federal government that may last from six to eight years, depending upon their good behavior. The parents of the bride, social leaders throughout most of Grand Traverse County, were accompanied by their personal banker and official photographer.

The Rev. I. Norman Shuttleworth, who has officiated at the weddings of Rockefellers, Vanderbilts, and other families listed in the New York Social Register, performed the Episcopalian ceremony at St. Christopher's Church in Southhampton, Long Island. Lou Mozart, organist at the Roxy Theater in New York City, played the march that he composed especially for the wedding and which he will also perform during intermissions at his theater's next all-star attraction—*I Married a Mobster*, starring Mae Murray, John Gilbert and Wallace Beery. The choir was augmented by the chorus of six sopranos and four contraltos from Le Strip Joint, a Hollywood café in which the groom is a silent partner. The three partners of record were recently found dead in an alley in Reno, Nevada.

Mrs. Gatsby, 32, graduated with distinction from the Lady Chesterfield Finishing School in Arlington Heights. She became a widow last year when her husband, Thomas Buchanan of West Egg, Long Island, was shot and killed in the Palm Court of the Plaza Hotel in New York City by George Wilson, the husband of his mistress, Myrtle Wilson. Mrs. Gatsby and Mrs. Wilson had met at the funeral of the late Mr. Wilson, and are currently collaborating on *Spanish Omelet*, a novel based on social activities in West Egg and adjacent towns in Long Island.

Mr. Gatsby, 34, graduated from East Shade Community College and then, according to the unconfirmed report of his private secretary, received an M.B.A. from Columbia University, and a Ph.D. from both Oxford and Cambridge, where he acquired the British accent and phraseology that he employs when being interviewed by upscale publications. At the last-named seat of higher learning, he, and his ghost writer, won the James Boswell Prize for his biography of Horatio Alger, from whose novels he had learned the virtues of thrift, hard work, and sharing his material blessings with the police and other figures in authority. He was an early supporter of former Presidents Harding and Coolidge, and signed photographs of the two statesmen hang in his den beside the trophies of his African safaris and of his triumphs in such upper-class diversions as polo, golf, contract bridge, tennis, croquet and adultery.

Because of the stock market panic on Wall Street, President Hoover, to whose campaign Mr. Gatsby had contributed a generous check, was unable to attend the wedding, but he sent a signed photograph of himself and Mrs. Hoover, and also an invitation to the newlyweds to drop in at the White House when they are next in Washington. The President suggested that they avoid Thursday afternoons, when he meets regularly with F.B.I. Director J. Edgar Hoover, who has a photographic memory for the faces in man-wanted posters.

THE HARDY FAMILY MOVIE SERIES

POLLY BROWN AND ANDREW HARDY

Polly Frances Brown, the daughter of Eleanor and Martin Brown of Walnut Hill, was married last evening to Andrew Richard Hardy, the son of Linda Hardy and U.S. Supreme Court Justice James Zachary Hardy of both Walnut Hill and Washington, D.C. Justice Hardy was elevated by President Truman soon after his famous decision in Walnut Hill Department of Environmental Protection vs. the Proctor Family, who started to barbecue smoked sausages on their front lawn on the Fourth of July and were still going strong on Labor Day.

The ceremony was performed at the Strawberry Street Baptist Church by the Rev. George Appleton, who was once the Sunday school teacher of both the bride and groom. The outdoor reception was in the rose garden of the Maison Lafayette on Main Street, where, when it was still Frenchie's Ice Cream Parlor, the former Miss Brown and Mr. Hardy used to enjoy a milk shake together, often from twin straws, after viewing a double feature at the Zenith Theater around the corner.

Mrs. Hardy, 24, majored in library science at Forest City College, where she graduated summa cum laude and was elected to Phi Beta Kappa. She is executive director of the Anita Van Drew Foundation, which distributes books and other educational materials to handicapped children and shut-ins throughout the country. Her parents retired recently after running Brown's Shoe Store for twenty years without a single complaint of a bad fit or even a corn or callous.

Mr. Hardy, 26, is the youngest district attorney in the history of the state, and Gov. Lawrence Franklin predicts that he will one day become the youngest justice on his dad's court in the nation's capital. Long interested solely in the maintenance of automobiles, especially roadsters, he was eventually convinced by his parents and sister Cecilia and Aunt Marion that the maintenance of law and order and family values in America was even more important. He graduated from Forest City College and received his law degree from Yale, where, as editor of the *Law Review,* he encouraged the publication of articles that dealt with the concerns of small-town Americans as well as the millionaire embezzlers and Wall Street corporations that will eventually employ Yale graduates.

Mr. and Mrs. Hardy will devote part of their honeymoon to an automobile tour of New England, where they have long desired to view the autumn foliage. They will drive the 1923 Stutz Bearcat that Mr. Hardy once reconstructed from parts found in junkyards and garages. While in the area of Wallingford, Connecticut, they will accept a longtime invitation and have their double portrait painted by Norman Rockwell, famed cover illustrator of *The Saturday Evening Post*. Mr. Rockwell is undecided about their pose. He would like them to be smooching, but he very definitely will not have them lying in bed together.

A DOLL'S HOUSE

NORA HEINZ AND TORVALD HELMER

Nora Heinz, daughter of Mr. and Mrs. Knut Herdal of Grudstad, was remarried yesterday to Torvald Helmer, a son of Dr. and Mrs. Nils Helmer of Einhuss. The Rev. Ingmar Klafmann, the Lutheran pastor who married them previously seventeen years ago, performed the private ceremony in Oslo at A Doll's House, one of the popular tea shops, specializing in macaroons, that the bride has established throughout Norway and will soon be expanding to other areas in Scandinavia.

The bride, who will retain her own name, and whose age, she says, is as much her own affair as the disposition of her love and loyalty, left the bed and board of her husband in 1875, after accusing him of treating her as a child and not as a grown woman who was his social and intellectual equal. She emigrated the next year to the United States, where she changed her name to Heinz after enjoying the ketchup, beans and other superior products manufactured by a firm of that name.

Out West, in the mining town of Reno, Nevada, she obtained an immediate divorce upon swearing to a magistrate that her husband had interfered with her God-given and constitutional rights to life, liberty and the pursuit of happiness. Reno had many saloons and gambling dens, but not a single bakery that produced the sort of macaroons and other biscuits which she had always craved and which, also, had long been a source of contention between her and her husband. He, for a variety of puritanical and old-fashioned reasons that thwarted her full maturity and independence, would have preferred her to eat bread crusts without either butter or jam. Her establishment of the first A Doll's House in Reno was an instant success, and so successful, in fact, that the Chamber of Commerce named her its Woman of the Year, an honor that had always gone previously to entertainers at a notorious saloon called Lola's Joint.

Mr. Helmer, 44, admits that during their first marriage, he often accused his wife of being a spendthrift, and of overindulging in sweets, and of preferring to perform the tarantella, a lascivious Italian dance, rather than attend to such simple but essential household duties as caring for his wardrobe and their three young children, giving orders to the governess and tutor, and to the cook, maids and porter, and to renew his subscriptions to various newspapers and journals, and to keep a detailed account of their expenditures, and to send out Christmas and birthday cards, and to attend monthly meetings of the Norwegian Association for the Prevention of Cruelty to Reindeer, and to remember to pay their quarterly dues to their church so that Pastor Lunstrum would not glower in their direction during his popular sermons on the wages of sin and avarice. But after her abrupt departure for a place unknown, when she slammed the door so violently that he had to summon Gregor Alvasson, the local carpenter, he learned from Mr. Alvasson, who had had a similar experience, that a century after the American and the French revolutions, women all over Scandinavia were clamoring for a revolution of their own, one that would raise their status to that of the men in their class, society and country.

Mr. Helmer still loved his wife despite her domestic deficiencies and passion for macaroons. Eagerly, he read the feminist tracts that Mr. Alvasson had received from his wife. Though a skeptic at first, he came to agree with them completely, to the point of organizing protest marches in front of city hall and the governor's residence. He did not care at all when these public demonstrations began to affect not only his precious and hard-won reputation as a solid and conservative citizen but also his business career and his income.

His leading of a demonstration in front of the royal palace led to a fine of a million kroner. Unable to raise such a sum, he was about to lose his house to the Benevolent Mortgage Company when Nora, who had read abroad of his situation, returned to Oslo to pay the fine and also renew acquaintance with the valiant fighter for women's rights who had once been her domineering husband.

Because of the groom's former views on household thrift, Miss Heinz and Mr. Helmer never enjoyed a honeymoon after their first marriage, but this time they are planning a long visit to Copenhagen, where they are eager to visit the Tivoli Gardens. Knowing of the universal passion for the several varieties of sweet rolls called Danish in Copenhagen, Miss Heinz has high hopes for establishing there several of her tea shops. Since her return, Mr. Helmer has become increasingly impressed by his wife's sense of business, and he has begun to consider an early retirement from his own business affairs so that he can devote himself to running their household.

Because they were deserted by the bride in their infancy and early youth, the three children from their first and unsuccessful marriage refused to attend the ceremony. Miss Heinz applauds their disdain for convention, and says that she could not be more proud of them if they had sneaked into Stockholm Palace and distributed feminist literature to King Oscar and his ministers. To make sure that her children remain independent, she has disinherited them, and has stipulated in her will that her fortune be used to advance the freedom of women throughout Norway and the world.

THE LONE RANGER

COOING DOVE AND THE LONE RANGER

Cooing Dove, the daughter of Tall Bear and Running Cloud, was married yesterday in The Valley of the Spring Moon, located between the towns of Whiskey Bend and Adamsville in Wyoming, to The Lone Ranger, a son of the Lone Couple, proprietors of Forgotten Ranch about two miles northeast of Tucson in Arizona Territory. Leaping Cougar, chief of the Pawnee tribe, performed the traditional ceremony outside the tepee devoted to occasions pleasing to the Great Spirit.

Mrs. Lone Ranger, 21, is adept at all the arts and crafts of her tribe, especially weaving, and several of her blankets are in the permanent exhibit of the Brooklyn Museum, an institution that specializes in Native American art. She graduated cum laude from the Pawnee Institute of Bird and Fish Identification.

Mr. Lone Ranger, 29, majored in frontier security at Middlebury College at Berkeley, Missouri. He served with distinction with the Texas Rangers until, after a series of attacks upon covered wagons farther to the north and west, he felt a responsibility to expand his field of operations. When his longtime assistant, Mr. Tonto, a Pawnee brave, was wounded in an ambush outside Saloon City, Oklahoma, last year, Mr. Lone Ranger brought him back to his tribe for rest and recuperation, and it was there that he meet the former Miss Cooing Dove, Mr. Tonto's sister.

Mr. and Mrs. Lone Ranger will honeymoon in New Orleans when the groom and Tonto return from escorting fourteen covered wagons with asthmatic children to Clean Air, Montana.

ANNA KARENINA

ANNA KARENINA AND
DMITRI SERGEYEVICH VRONSKY

Anna Karenina, the daughter of Ivan Alexeyevich and Irina Denisov, was married yesterday to Count Dmitri Sergeyevich Vronsky, the son of Count Serge Pyotrovich and Charlotta Vronsky. The bride's father is a permanent senior chief counselor first class in Vitebst, and her mother is the heiress of Boris Zhokov, sole owner of the Proud Eagle Samovar Factory in Moscow. The groom's father earned immortality when, as general of Ivan the Terrible's Personal Cavalry, he led the glorious charge against the Turks at the Battle of Sevastapol in 1851. Archbishop Pyotr Grindov performed the ceremony at the Church of St. Vladimir in St. Petersburg. The choir of two hundred bassos from the groom's regiment was under the direction of Captain Misha Leontovitch Musoff.

The bride, who emerged from her period of mourning last month, is the widow of the late Alexei Karenin, long a pillar of society in St. Petersburg as well as a trusted and much esteemed senior adviser to His Supreme and Royal Highness the Czar. She is a graduate of the Baroness Valeria's Exclusive Academy for the Daughters of Devoted Subjects of the Czar. She received there a degree in household management and the discipline of serfs and other servants.

Two years ago, her interest in the Royal Siberian Relief Fund for the Victims of Frostbite brought her into intimate contact with Count Vronsky, whose family have been longtime patrons of the institution. When her husband learned of their deep and scandalous friendship, and demanded that she terminate it at once, she was too distraught to pray to her icon for divine guidance, and attempted suicide by stepping in front of a train. Due to a labor strike instigated by anarchists under the evil influence of Mikhail Bakunin, the 9:12 express to Moscow stopped running just as it pulled into her station, and her life was spared. In a typical act of mercy, the Czar exiled the anarchists and strikers to Siberia for only forty years.

The bride's husband at the time, Alexei Karenin, was less fortunate, however. As great as they were, his laudable passions for professional advancement and social respectability were exceeded by devotion to the House of Romanov, and when he learned of an anarchist plot to assassinate Czar Nicholas by poisoning his caviar, he singlehandedly raided their headquarters and was able to kill the ringleaders before he himself was shot in the back. Befitting his rank and achievement, he was buried with full fourth-class honors at the Royal Cemetery for Loyal Subjects in Tubirsk.

Count Vronsky graduated from the Peter the Great Military Academy, from which he received a master's degree in horsemanship and gambling. He and his bride will honeymoon on the French Riviera. In accordance with the vows they made during premarital counseling with Father Igor at the All Saints Monastery in Aspez, they will wear hairshirts until the Czar's birthday and reside in separate suites and practice chastity during their honeymoon on the French Riviera.

THE HEIDI STORIES

HEIDI SCHMIDT AND PETER WERNER

Heidi Schmidt, the daughter of the late Tobias and the late Adelheid Schmidt and the granddaughter of Johannes Schmidt, all from a hillside goat farm just above the friendly village of Dörfli in the Swiss Alps, was married yesterday to Peter Werner, son of the late Peter and the late Brigitte Werner, from a neighboring goat farm in the same area. Pastor Aloysius Xavier Keller of St. Agnes Church in Maienfeld performed the ceremony, which was accompanied by the wedding music from *Lohengrin* by Richard Wagner, who always enjoyed his morning lebkuchen with a generous topping of goat cheese. The special transcription for alpenhorn and goat bells was composed by Ludwig Muller, first alpenhornist with the Zurich Philharmonic and a devotee of all twelve goat cheeses from the Schmidt and Werner farms, which were merged last month.

Mrs. Werner, 24, is in charge of milking operations and cheese cultures on the farm, producers of Edelweiss Goat Yogurt and Yodel All-Natural Dairy Products. She received her master's degree from the University of Bern, where she majored in agricultural economics and discovered a new enzyme that her grandfather later developed into Angelica, a new light cheese without either sodium or cholesterol. Thanks to daily consumption of his new cheese, Grandfather Schmidt, 82, recently became the oldest successful climber of the Matterhorn.

Mr. Werner, 30, is the chief herdsman on the Schmidt-Warner Farm, and also an evening student at the University of Gratz, where he is majoring in environmental studies in the hope that he will one day develop a process to can or bottle the fresh mountain air and then offer it for sale in urban areas that are subject to air pollution.

The bride and groom will vacation on the Italian Riviera in the villa of Baron Gottfried von Kerner. The baroness is the former Klara Sesemann of Frankfurt, whom Heidi and Peter befriended and inspired in childhood when she was lonely, paralyzed, and much depressed by the slow progress of a medical treatment that neglected her spirit and morale. Baroness Klara won the gold medal in cross-country skiing in the most recent winter Olympic games in Norway, and her wedding present to the dear friends responsible for her physical and spiritual rehabilitation will be the establishment in Dörfli of the Heidi and Peter Free Clinic for Children and Goats.

THE GRAPES OF WRATH and OF MICE AND MEN

AMY SUE JOAD AND GEORGE MILTON

Amy Sue Joad, a daughter of Mr. and Mrs. Hank Joad of North Monterey, was married yesterday in Laguna Junction to George Milton, a son of the late Irene and Jacob Milton. The groom's parents resided in Trailer City, Nevada, until their residence was carried away by a flood. The ceremony, frequently interrupted by sandstorms, was performed by the Rev. Terry Joad, a cousin of the bride, outside the Church of Abiding Hope, which was repossessed immediately afterward by the First National Bank of California. During an impromptu sermon, the Rev. Joad predicted the failure of the best-laid schemes of California banks as well as those of mice and of poor farm hands like the groom and his late partner Lennie Small.

Mrs. Milton, 32, is in charge of Counseling Services at the California Department of Correction. After attending night classes for ten years while working as a waitress seven days a week to support not only nine siblings but her also handicapped parents, she graduated cum laude from the University of California at Berkeley, where she received a master's degree in the rehabilitation of prison inmates who were victims of the excesses of capitalism in America.

Mr. Milton, 35, had no formal education after an altercation with Mr. James Grubb, his kindergarten teacher at P.S. ½ in South Salinas. Mr. Grubb had attempted to whip him for coming to school with dirty hands because his parents, both unemployed, could not afford to buy soap. He and his late friend Lennie Small, also a dropout from P.S. ½, were tramps and migratory farm workers for many years. When Mr. Small, mentally challenged and long in need of the psychotherapy that only the rich can afford, accidentally killed the wife of Curley, their sadistic employer, Mr. Milton in turn killed Mr. Small in a supreme act of friendship because he feared the exactions of law and society.

Mr. Milton's counselor at Soledad State Prison was the former Miss Joad, and she not only treated his emotional problems but also helped him secure a commutation of sentence to the three years he had already served. Mr. Milton took full advantage of the prison library, and he not only obtained the equivalency of a college education but also wrote a memoir, *Even a Hobo Can Hope*, which has already been sold to Random House and has been optioned by M.G.M. for a motion picture with June Allyson, Van Johnson, Elizabeth Taylor and Robert Walker.

Mr. and Mrs. Milton will honeymoon in Las Vegas, where Mrs. Milton has been asked by the Mayo Clinic to establish a regional center for the treatment of compulsive gambling. Mr. Milton, currently a spokesman for the Burpee Seed Company, has been invited to speak at the formal opening of the Princess Jasmine Rose Garden at the Aladdin Hotel.

THE WORLD OF JEEVES and
BERTIE WOOSTER

THE HONORABLE FIDELIA COYLE AND
JEEVES, THE 17TH DUKE OF BEDDINGHURST

Fidelia Penelope Imogene Sandra Coyle, the daughter of the Earl and Countess of Chiddington, was married yesterday in Upper Selborne in Hampshire to Jeeves, the son and heir of the late Duke and Duchess of Beddinghurst. The bride's father, in addition to being a senior director both of Lloyd's of London and the Bank of England, is president of the Chaddington Cricket Club, which was founded by an ancestor in 1330, after an earlier ancestor had invented the game of cricket in 1300. The bride's mother, the Countess Alicia, is a lady in waiting to the Queen and also a consultant in Ceylon tea and marmalade at Selfridge's in London.

Maxwell Saunders, the Archbishop of Canterbury and a maternal uncle of the groom, performed the ceremony at All Saints Church in South Selborne, where the family has worshiped since the arrival in

Hampshire of an ancestor, Randolph the Peaceful, in 1067. His name had been the Randolph the Conqueror until the invasion in 1066 of William the Conqueror, whose army was five times as large.

Minutes before the beginning of the wedding procession and of the epithalamium, "Pomp and Matrimony," written by Sir Milton Mildew, soprano Angelica de Lammermoor, who had performed earlier in the day a program of birdcalls for the BBC, came down with laryngitis and had to be replaced by Tessie Owens, who often sings popular ballads Saturday night at the Roaring Lion, a pub in Wittingham. She had no time to learn Sir Milton's composition, even if she were able to read music, and she performed instead one of her ever-popular offerings at the Roaring Lion, "If You Happen to Meet My Charlie, Don't Lend Him a Farthing for Beer."

The new Duchess of Beddinghurst, 25, made her social debut in the ballroom of Wellstone Manor in Derbyshire, the ancestral home of the Duke and Duchess of Derby. She studied her pedigree at the Royal College of Genealogy in Greenwich and was later a drama critic with *Mews and Manor*, a periodical devoted to the gracious living that she has always exemplified. While working on an article about the plays of Oscar Wilde and Gilbert and Sullivan, she discovered that the misplacement of babies in Victoria Station and other public places was not uncommon with members of the gentry who, after riding to the hounds more than once a week, often contracted Squire Tettington's syndrome, a disturbance of certain neurons in the frontal lobes of the cerebellum. Her investigations into the phenomenon led to an introduction to her future husband, who, under the name of Jeeves, and unaware of his distinguished ancestry, was serving with hereditary excellence as valet-butler to Mr. Bertram Wooster, Esq., a gentleman of leisure who resided at 12 Charlton Walk in Mayfair and was an original member of the Drones Club.

Mr. Jeeves, 37, as Daniel Roderick Percival, the 17th Duke of Beddinghurst, still prefers to be called after bearing the briefer cognomen since his elevation to the status of senior butler, learned the domestic arts and sciences from his adopted parents, Barney and Daffodil Jeeves, who had served at the residences of Lord and Lady Paddington and other members of the gentry and aristocracy. His rapid rise from scullery boy at the semi-detached Surrey manor of a parvenu brewer to valet-butler to Mr. Wooster, his final and most demanding employer, was once the subject of an article in *The Domestic Times of London*. He has declined the honor of being proposed for the Drones

Club by his former employer, and as his final service, he imparted to his successor not only the secret recipe for his famous hot toddy but also his even more famous restorative after an overindulgence in the hot toddy.

Before taking up residence at Waverly Court, their estate in Beddinghurst that was rebuilt by Sir Christopher Wren in 1720, the newlyweds will honeymoon at Windsor Lodge, one of the groom's summer homes, located on the Isle of Wight. There he will be within a short stroll of Windsor Royal, one of the King's summer homes, of which he has heard through the butler's "grapevine" that the silverware is not always polished to a brilliance that will merit complete satisfaction. As a peer of the realm, and one whose family motto has always been "Duty or Dishonor," he will be ready, if necessary, to offer both advice and an elbow to his former colleagues at Windsor Royal.

BRIEF ENCOUNTER

LAURA MARGARET LINDSEY AND DR. ALEC WINFIELD

In a ceremony almost as brief as their romantic encounter had once threatened to become, Laura Margaret Lindsey, the precious daughter of Major and Mrs. Lyle Partridge, was married yesterday to Dr. Alec Winfield, a son of Cynthia and Dr. Oliver Winfield, the head of ophthalmology at St. Bartholomew's Hospital in London. The ceremony had been scheduled for the last Sunday in May, but because the Royal Medical Society had requested the groom to organize an emergency program to deal with an outbreak of tonsillitis in Kenya, the Rev. Thomas Gordon, a cousin of the bride, performed the hastily scheduled ceremony in his rectory at St. Mary's Church in Little Hasley in Oxfordshire.

The ceremony was restricted to the immediate family and a few close friends, and in attendance were Mr. Gregory Lindsey, the bride's former husband, and Mrs. Gertrude Winfield, the groom's former wife. Though the newlyweds, while still married to their former spouses, were discreet about the chaste but passionate relationship that had developed after their chance encounter in the snack bar at the railroad station in Leamington Spa, Mr. Lindsey and the first Mrs. Winfield were able to detect a change in conjugal ardor in their otherwise satisfactory lower-upper middle-class homes in Yelford and Brighthampton, respectively.

By a happy coincidence, they both subscribed to *Better Shrubs and Marigolds*, where they came across an advertisement that urged them to seek guidance from Happily Ever After, a marital counseling service in North Exeter. Just before their first appointment with a counselor, they met there in the waiting room, hit it off at once like fish and chips, and decided right then and there to cancel their appointments, divorce Laura and Alec, their current spouses, and marry each other. They will wed next Sunday, but postpone their honeymoon in Greece till after the gardening season.

Alec and Laura Winfield plan a brief honeymoon in Edinburgh and the Highlands, but rather than drive there, they will, despite the inconvenience and frequent change of trains, travel by railroad, and set out from the station where they met and fell eternally in love. Informed after the wedding ceremony that the snack bar at the station is now a McDonald's fast-food restaurant, and that they can no longer obtain and enjoy at leisure their usual rock buns and Typhoo tea with just a dash of milk but no sugar, they replied that they now had each other for life, and that would be even more refreshing and satisfactory.

GREAT EXPECTATIONS and
A TALE OF TWO CITIES

OLIVIA CONSTANCE HAVERSHAM AND
SYDNEY HAROLD CARTON

In a fulfillment of her long-delayed great expectation to be one in body and spirit with an English gentleman, Olivia Constance Haversham, the daughter of Mr. and Mrs. Reginald Haversham of Satis House in Somersetshire, was married yesterday to Sydney Harold Carton, a son of the late Colonel and Mrs. Lamson Carton of Lower Feebish in Dorset. Canon Albert Gillespie, a former Rugby classmate of the groom, conducted the High Episcopalian ceremony at Lincoln's Inn Chapel in London. Sir Lawrence Diggs, Master of the Queen's Music, performed on the organ that was built in 1640 and was once played by Handel and Mozart.

The bride, 42, studied advanced embroidery with her governess, Sally Osborne, and French and the flute with her tutor, Madame Genevieve La Porte. For a long time she was engaged to Sir Claude Mayfair. During that period her principal chaperone was her aunt, Mrs. Sophia Wentworth of Royal Booley in Shropshire. When Sir Claude failed to appear for the ceremony on their wedding day, nor even send an explanation of his absence, she became a recluse and stopped the clocks in her house. Her hatred of men became so intense that she trained her lovely ward, Estella Banks, to entice and break the hearts of Pip Pirrip and all the other men she met.

The bridegroom, 50, graduated summa cum laude from Trinity College at Cambridge, where he also won the coveted Edward Gibbon Prize for his treatise on the French monarchy, in which he predicted its fall and replacement by a popular government that would be even more ruthless. Unlike Queen Marie Antoinette, its First Lady would not be so compassionate as to advise starving citizens without bread to eat cake instead.

After coming down from Cambridge, the bridegroom studied at Lincoln's Inn in the chambers of Frederick Snip, K.C., and eventually he became one of the most popular barristers in the kingdom. The French Revolution and subsequent Reign of Terror came as no surprise to Mr. Carton, and when Charles Darnay, his successful rival for the hand of Lucie Mannette, was falsely accused of treason and sentenced to death, Mr. Carton appealed to the Lord Chancellor for a postponement in his current trial at the Old Bailey, and then he rushed off to Paris and took the place of Mr. Darney, whom he much resembled, on the guillotine. Not a moment too soon, he was rescued, according to plan, by another old boy from Rugby, Sir Percival Blakeley, also known to intimate friends as the Scarlet Pimpernel.

Mr. Carton met his bride-to-be not long after he was offered a brief to defend her former fiancé, Sir Claude Mayfair, on a charge of breach of promise by Lady Cecilia Stanton of Great Misshapenden. When, during his early inquiries, he learned that Sir Claude had once jilted seven other women, among them Miss Haversham, he not only refused the brief but supplied Lord Chief Justice Rupert Knox with the information that later convicted Sir Claude of no less than seventeen criminal charges, including ten for bigamy and four for cheating at whist and cribbage, and had him deported to Australia for ninety-nine years.

After much turbulence in their lives, Miss Haversham's ward, Estella Banks, had married Pip Pirrip. Wishing to share their marital felicity, the happy young couple finally persuaded Miss Haversham to emerge from her long seclusion and meet Mr. Carton at a tea shop in Bath. His punctuality, and his apparent indifference to her consumption of all of the cucumber sandwiches and most of the Queen Anne biscuits, clotted cream and strawberries were able to convince her that there yet remained a man of honor in England.

KING KONG

LADY BONG ANN DIANE AND
HRH KING KONG

The Lady Bong Ann Diane, a daughter of Count Ping and Countess Pong of Shinbone Island, was married yesterday on Skull Island to her cousin twice removed, His Highness King Kong, a son of Dowager Queen Mong and the late King Fong. The Rev. E. Kenneth Winyard, a Methodist missionary, officiated atop a forty-foot ladder in an outdoor ceremony at Terrace on the Hill.

Queen Bong, 24, is president and chairwoman of the Royal Society for the Elimination of Ticks and Mosquitoes, one of her family's many philanthropies on Shinbone Island and throughout the archipelago. Her family has been prominent on Shinbone Island since their arrival centuries ago in the retinue of the current King Kong's illustrious ancestor, King William Kong the Conqueror. She graduated cum laude from St. Simian College in New York, where she majored in inter-species relationships, a course initiated in her honor. She will keep her maiden name, so that classmates will be sure to remember her when she returns for class reunions.

King Kong, 25, was majoring in genealogy at Yarvard University on Humerus Island until he had to interrupt his education in order to lead his subjects in defending their homeland from an invasion of dinosaurs led by Tyrannosaurus Rex 3rd of Kneebone Island. In his capacity of Overseer of the Royal Coffers, which provides revenue not only for the defense of his realm but for the maintenance of its wading and swimming pools, its forest trails, social security and national health plan, he regularly tours Skull Island to collect taxes from humans and other species. His encounter with Ann Darrell, an aspiring actress specializing in melodrama, and with her associates Carl Denim and Jack Driscoll, led to an unscheduled ocean voyage to the United States and a visit to the top of the Empire State Building in New York City. His fall from the building, caused by aircraft in the employ of an enemy of the Skull Island way of life, would have eventuated in tragedy but for the timely services of Dr. David W. Cohen, head of the Institute of Tropical and Macromedical Studies at Beth Israel Hospital. Upon his return to Skull Island, His Majesty's first acts were to send his benefactor a bunch of deluxe organic bananas and, of course, his national health insurance forms.

The newlyweds will honeymoon in New York City, where, combining affairs of state with pleasure, the King wishes to correct any wrong impression he may have made on his previous visit, when he succumbed to an unusually severe case of culture shock and destroyed property whose owners were later fully compensated by the Desert and Jungle Insurance Company. After New York City, the royal couple will visit Niagara Falls, under which they have long wished to enjoy a leisurely shower.

THE STRANGE CASE OF DR. JEKYLL
AND MR. HYDE

SERENA DONALDSON AND DR. HENRY JEKYLL

Serena Muriel Donaldson, a daughter of the Rev. Julian and Mrs. Henrietta Donaldson of Mayfair in London, was married yesterday to Henry Jekyll, M.D., D.C.L., LL.D., F.R.S., in London. He is the son of Julia and Ronald Jekyll, both of them deceased and resting peacefully together in an exclusive and most desirable section of Kensal Green Cemetery. The bride's father, who is president of the Royal Society for the Propagation of Christian Knowledge and Morality, performed the ceremony at St. Brigit's Church on Pimlico Road, which is the headquarters of the worldwide organization. The bride's mother, a cousin of Sir Glenville Shack, curator of Regency pottery at the Victoria and Albert Museum, is secretary-treasurer of the same organization. Last June, both parents were honored with an invitation to the three-thirty o'clock tea on the lawn of Buckingham Palace. There, Her Majesty Queen Victoria directed quite a bright smile in their general direction.

The bride, who once recruited Emmeline Pankhurst in the struggle for women's rights, believes that one of those rights is the withholding of her age from newspaper personnel and other strangers. She studied nursing under Florence Nightingale at St. Thomas's Hospital. Much influenced by her parents, she has made it a practice to treat not only the physical symptoms of her patients but also the shortcomings in their religion and morality. While in the Orient to establish modern nursing schools under the aegis of the Nightingale Society, she mastered the science of judo, and has found it invaluable in subduing mental patients whose multiple personalities include one or more with an affinity for violence. Never did her skill prove more providential when, in the course of a late-night visit to an outpatient in Shoreditch, she was savagely assaulted by a Mr. Edward Hyde in an alley off Hoxton Street. When she retaliated and smashed his skull with the judo blow called, in English, "thunderstorm in garden of peonies," he remained unconscious for twenty hours, but upon his awakening was a completely new and more congenial man, to the extent of contributing a thousand guineas to the Royal Society for the Propagation of Christian Knowledge and Morality.

The groom, 42, graduated with honors from St. Bartholomew's Medical College and was later both an instructor and a senior internist at the Foundling Hospital in Coram's Fields. While serving as chief neurologist at the National Hospital for Nervous Disorders, he initiated a series of novel experiments in a secluded laboratory at home. First on animals and then on himself, he attempted to identify the brain centers that govern morality, character, personality, and loyalty to the Royal Family in general and to Queen Victoria in particular. To expedite his work, which he hoped to finish in time for a monograph upon the occasion of the Queen's biennial visit to the Royal College of Brain Surgeons, he began to experiment upon himself with an ever more potent mixture of chemicals that ultimately proved detrimental to his sense of good and evil. Also, the chemicals distorted the handsome features that were painted more than once by John Singer Sargent, world famous for his portrait of Madame X, the most elegant woman of her day.

The bride will retain her maiden name, and also the keys to the groom's laboratory in their new residence.

THE TALES OF ROBIN HOOD
AND HIS MERRY MEN

THE MAID MARION AND ROBIN HOOD

The Maid Marion, who is listed in *Damsels of the Realm* as Marion Martha Hope, the youngest daughter of the Earl and Countess of Exmoor, was married yesterday to Robin Hood, who, to confuse the enemies of both himself and of England, is listed in the same compendium of the nobility as both the Earl of Huntingdon and the Earl of Locksley. The ceremony, in a clearing in Sherwood Forest, was performed by Friar Tuck. Until he fled religious persecution and became one of Robin Hood's so-called Merry Men, Friar Tuck was the priest at St. Anselm's Church in Nottingham, a structure destroyed by King John and his local agent, the Sheriff, because its architecture was Anglo Saxon rather than Norman.

The Maid Marion, 18, studied her catechism and then post-flagellation nursing at the nunnery of the Sisters of St. Ernestine until it was ordered destroyed by the Sheriff after a false allegation that the

Sisters had prepared a mutton stew within days of the disappearance of a royal sheep in Sherwood Forest. Further, according to the Sheriff, the stew had been consumed on a Friday, a day when the church decrees the eating of fish rather than meat.

Robin Hood, 21, studied archery and fencing with members of his father's guard, and his skills stood him in good stead when he fled to the relative safety of Sherwood Forest after being revealed as a supporter of the legitimate king of England, Richard the Lion-Hearted. He denies the charges of usurper King John that his taking from the rich and giving to the poor will destroy all business incentive and turn England into an atheistic and tyrannical welfare state, a despotism even worse than the one recently established in Moscovy by the Czar Mischa the Terrible.

The wedding banquet was disturbed briefly when Alan O'Dale announced that the Sheriff and his men were on their way, furious at the theft of the king's largest pedigree boar. Because the boar on the spit was huge and not quite done, Robin requested his bride to continue turning it while he and his Merry Men set off to dispose of their uninvited guests.

THE THIRD MAN

ANNA SCHMIDT AND HOLLY MARTINS

After a brief interruption during which military police of the occupying forces searched for the third man involved in the theft of a cuckoo clock from the Schonbrunn Palace, Anna Theresa Schmidt, a daughter of Mr. and Mrs. Heinrich Schmidt of Prague, was married yesterday to Holly Martins, the son of Mr. and Mrs. Andrew Martins of Kansas City, Missouri. Father Heinrich Schmoot, a longtime acquaintance of the bride, performed the ceremony at All Saints Church in Vienna.

The bride, 33, studied social work at Eastern Prague College and was an assistant director of the personnel department at the Skoda Steel Factory in Pilsen. Early in 1945, while she was in Vienna for the funeral of her grandfather, Wilhelm Leimer, a former flutist with the Vienna Philharmonic, units of the Russian army encircled the city and she was unable to return home. With the assistance of Harry Lime, an American entrepreneur who specialized in the import and distribution of pharmaceuticals, she was able to find an apartment and also a job with a theatrical group. She later became the *Liebling* of Mr. Lime, and continued the relationship despite frequent rumors that he had criminal connections and dabbled in the black market. When Mr. Lime was reportedly killed in an auto accident, she wanted to return to Prague, but passport difficulties always prevented her departure.

The bridegroom, 40, graduated from the Famous Writers Correspondence School and was a reporter for several years with the *Kansas City Star-Sentinel* and other newspapers in the region. After the success of his book, *The Return of the Sacramento Kid*, he became a full-time writer of Western novels. During a visit to Vienna after the war, he attempted to renew acquaintance with his boyhood friend, Mr. Lime, and learned from Major Calloway of the British Occupation Force that Mr. Lime was dead, and that he had been a distributor of contaminated penicillin which had killed dozens of invalids, mostly children.

Mr. Martins had the instincts of both a journalist and a novelist, and they enabled him, with the assistance of Major Calloway, to discover that Mr. Lime was still alive and hiding somewhere in Vienna. They set a trap for Mr. Lime, and he was eventually shot and killed after a pursuit through the sewers.

The wedding march was performed on the zither by Johann Weber. More used to playing on the sidewalk outside the Cafe Mozart on the Prater Platz, Mr. Weber was much disappointed when congregants and members of the wedding party did not throw coins into the top hat that he had borrowed for the upscale occasion from a doorman friend at the Grand Hotel Wien.

At one point in the ceremony, a cat entered the church and proceeded along the nave and up to the altar, where it began to lick the shoes of Father Schmoot. He winked at the animal as if they shared a secret unknown to Major Calloway and the bride and groom.

THE CASTLE

FRIEDA KOVACS AND K.

Frieda Kovacs, the daughter of Johann and Ernestine Kovacs, was married yesterday to K., the son of Mr. and Mrs. K. of Prague, in an outdoor ceremony across a moat from the Castle of Count West-west outside Dvorsk. The groom's parents, whom he has not met since infancy because they live on another floor in a vast apartment building without a directory or concierge, were unable to attend because they had to stay home to catalog the contents of their pantry after the mysterious disappearance of a can of sauerkraut in a neighbor's apartment.

The ceremony was performed by a functionary who would not identify his or her name, sex or religious affiliation, if any. When asked by the bride and groom for their certificate of marriage, the functionary replied that the registrar at the local Bureau of Licenses had run out of ink and paper three years ago, but that they were on order from the Ministry of Minor Purchases and were expected to arrive at any time, if not today then within a month or year.

Mrs. K., 27, is a barmaid at the Asp and Scorpion, a tavern in the village of Wenzel near the Castle. She learned her skills from her parents, also bar personnel, and her catechism at St. Rudolph's Church, which used to grace the town square until it disappeared one night during a thunderstorm. Later, during another storm, it reappeared two thousand miles away at the foot of Mount Sinai in Palestine. Mrs. K. and other townspeople made a pilgrimage to their old church at its new location, but by that time it had moved to the Himalayas.

Mr. K., 32, double-majored in mathematics and medieval architecture at the University of Prague, where he was named an Albrecht scholar and received a full scholarship to the Royal College of Surveying, from which he graduated cum laude. He was an adjunct professor of surveying at Providence College in Vinding until he arrived one day for work and learned that the ancient institution, established in 704 by King Jan the Virtuous, had closed its doors forever because the bursar had invested the endowment fund in a Parisian brothel which had gone bankrupt. He is currently the surveyor at the castle of Count West-west, where he has been unable to gain admittance or even communicate with Count West-west or any of his personnel.

The newlyweds are honeymooning in the town of Old Krushna near the Castle. Early in their engagement, they had paid the Cupid Travel Agency in Prague for a two-week honeymoon package tour of Italy that included eight days and one night at the Paradiso Hotel in Venice. Only the brochures and maps of their trip ever arrived, and when Mr. K. phoned the travel agency for his missing train tickets and hotel vouchers, the long-distance operator, a Mongolian with a rudimentary command of Czech, informed him that no such firm had ever existed in Prague.

THE PRISONER OF ZENDA

HRH PRINCESS FLAVIA AND RUDOLF RASSENDYLL

The Princess Flavia Olivia Elizabeth, a daughter of the Duke Maximilian Ludwig and the Duchess Carmela Natalia of Ruritania, was married late yesterday during a glorious sunset to Rudolf Rassendyll, the son of General Anthony and Lady Amelia Rassendyll of London, Surrey, Edinburgh, Bermuda, Kenya and India. At the command of HRH Queen Victoria, the Most Reverend Charles Winfield Marshall, Archbishop of Canterbury, performed the ceremony at St. Paul's Cathedral in London. In honor of the occasion, Sir Edward Elgar composed a wedding march that he called, with his customary wit as well as musical genius, "Pomp and Impersonation."

The bride, 25, graduated magna cum laude from the Gertstenberg College for Women in Cologne. Like her mother and grandmother before her, she was valedictorian of her class, and the title of her address was, "What Every Princess Can Learn from the

Military Campaigns of Frederick the Great of Prussia."
She heads the social service department at St. Bertha's
Hospital for Royal Blood Disorders in Zenda, a town in
Ruritania. Her father, the Duke Maximilian, attended
the ceremony in a wheelchair that was propelled by his
coachman and two footmen. The previous week, during
a class reunion at Heidelberg College, the Duke and an
old classmate, Count Rupert of Vettmach-on-Moselle,
decided to fence with sabers and augment their famous
collections of scars, immortalized in *The Von Gitlitzer
Book of Records*. Even with the aid of a monocle, Count
Rupert's eyesight was not what it was forty years ago,
and he cut the Duke severely on both legs. The Duke
was too much of a nobleman, and sportsman, to make
a fuss about the matter, and he insisted that the match
continue to the end of the twenty-eight minutes that
are mandated by the rules of the Baron von Münster.

The bridegroom, 33, attended All Souls College
in Oxford. There he majored in English history, and
one of his tutorials, "Foxhunting in the North Riding
of Yorkshire from 1627 to 1837," the year of Victoria's
ascendancy, was later expanded and published by
the world-famous firm of Macmillan. The book
was commended by the Prince of Wales, who later
became his friend and patron. He is currently engaged
on *Tallyho*, a twelve-volume guide to foxhunting

throughout the British Isles, and the first volume, devoted to the home counties, has already become so indispensable to sportsmen that the Prince of Wales avers that he, his gamekeepers and hunting parties will never leave Sandringham Palace without it. Nor, to be sure, without their customary flasks of whisky, gin or brandy, according to taste.

The bride was previously engaged to the bridegroom's distant cousin, King Rudolf of Ruritania, whom he much resembles. The marriage had been arranged in her infancy, for reasons of state, but though she respected Prince Rudolf as her future sovereign, she could not bring herself to love him as a man. Prince Rudolf had a half-brother, Duke Michael of Strelsau, and in an attempt to usurp the throne, Duke Michael kidnapped Prince Rudolf before his coronation, and he imprisoned him in his hunting lodge in Zenda.

Loyal to the prince, Fritz von Tarlenheim, persuaded the groom to substitute for his cousin during the coronation and other ceremonies. In the course of his impersonation, the groom met the Princess Flavia, and he fell deeply and eternally in love with her, but personal honor as well as the political stability of Ruritania and the Balkans forbad him to reveal his true identity.

After being rescued by the groom and other

supporters, King Rudolf immediately demanded of Flavia that they set an early date for their wedding. Though he lacked the graces of the man she had come to love in recent weeks, her honor as a member of the House of Bloomengarten forced her to accede to him. Fortunately, on the eve of the wedding, she was visited by Flavia von Graffman, a distant cousin from Milwaukee, Wisconsin. Flavia von Graffman, who resembled the Princess Flavia as much as Rudolf Rassendyll did King Rudolf, had long loved King Rudolf from afar, ever since seeing a picture postcard of him upon his Lipizzan stallion, and ultimately, with the assistance of Princess Flavia and the ever helpful Fritz von Tarlenheim, she married King Rudolf while Princess Flavia became engaged to her true love, Rudolf Rassendyll.

To avoid confusion among both royalty and commoners, the two couples have promised that they will always live in palaces and castles that are far apart, and that their yachts will never be in the same ocean at the same time.

The bridegroom is a cousin of Sir Basil Rassendyll, who, while governor of British colonies in the Caribbean, invented the comfortable garment that was known as Rassendyll shorts until, because of frequent misspellings, the name was eventually changed to Bermuda shorts.

THE LITTLE MERMAID

PRINCESS MELINDA AND PRINCE ALASTON

The Princess Melinda, the youngest and most petite of the six mermaid daughters of King Marlin and Queen Albacore of Coralia, located south of Finland at the bottom of the Baltic Sea, was married last evening to Prince Alaston, the handsome son of King Gerald and Queen Roberta of Hollendorf. Bishop Sigmund Wallstein performed the ceremony at the Stefankirche in Hesstoff-on-the-Rhine, where the groom's parents spend their summer vacations when they cannot agree upon their seaside retreat on the French Riviera or their mountain lodge in the Swiss Alps. In honor of the occasion, Johannes Bombeimer, the kapellmeister royal, composed and personally conducted a composition called "Fanfare and Fugue for Twelve Glockenspiels."

The Princess Melinda, 20, is vice president in charge of fund-raising for the International Association for the Prevention of Cruelty to Sea Life. She graduated from Father Neptune University in

New South Whales, where she majored in marine biology. Her flower decorations upon the driftwood of wrecked ships are in the permanent collection of the Bass Museum in Boston, and her book of poems, *Driftwood Dreams*, has been praised by British Poet Laureate Alfred Lord Tennyson and other critics as the best work of maritime literature since *Moby Dick* if not "The Rime of the Ancient Mariner."

Prince Alaston, 26, has recently been promoted to rear admiral in the small but highly efficient fleet of his country. Taking advantage of one of the provisions of a friendship pact with the United States, which his country helped free from British oppression in 1781, he was able to attend and graduate from the prestigious naval academy at Annapolis. At the conclusion of commencement exercises there, he would have wished to follow his country's ancient custom upon such a happy occasion, and have thrown a wineglass into the air. Because the Naval Academy disapproved of wine and wineglasses, he threw up his cap instead. His example was followed by his classmates, and the throwing of hats is now an essential part of commencement exercises at all American military academies.

Because she was a mermaid and the prince a human, Princess Melinda believed for a long time that her deep and undying love for him was doomed to tragedy. Though she had saved his life in a storm at sea, his immediate failure to return her affection led her to consult Dr. Ruth Butterfish, the royal marriage counselor, who told her: "Alas, my dear, fins and feet can never meet." Fortunately, while the princess was composing a suicide note on her favorite rock, a wind came along and blew the note onto the deck of *The Singing Swan*, a marine research vessel under the command of Professor Hugo Pettenkofer of Kaiser Wilhelm University in Berlin. Thanks to a generous grant from Chancellor Bismarck of Prussia, the professor was adept in the new science of genetics, and after a brief and painless surgical procedure, he enabled the princess and her prince to effect a happy medium in their lower anatomies that eliminated any physical and procreational impediments to their marriage. But every golden sunset has a dark cloud, as we learn again and again from Danish philosopher Soren Kierkegaard, and the International Olympic Committee has ruled that, because of their physical advantage, the royal couple may not participate in any future swimming events.

The newlyweds will spend their honeymoon at, appropriately, the Lord Nelson Hotel at Clacton-on-Sea in Essex, England. From there, they will swim the Stour and other waterways to Cambridge

University, where the bride is scheduled to deliver the annual Lord Humphrey Sackville Memorial Lecture on comparative linguistics. Her subject will be the resemblance between Middle English and the syntax of a certain school of dolphins who favor the waters near the Shetland Islands.

THE JANE MARPLE and HERCULE POIROT MYSTERY NOVELS

JANE MARPLE AND HERCULE POIROT

Jane Victoria Marple, the daughter of the late Vicar Andrew Albert Marple and the late Louise Jean May Marple, was married yesterday in St. Mary Mead in Surrey to Hercule Poirot, the son of the late Samson Poirot and the late Heloise Poirot. The Rev. Charles Pontwick performed the ceremony at St. Clement's Church, after which, during his benediction, he adjured the mature newlyweds, quoting the poet Robert Herrick, to "gather ye rosebuds while ye may."

Mrs. Poirot, who is old enough to recall a time when a woman's age was her own business and a coroner's, had no formal education beyond the age of eight, when she was dismissed from Queen Victoria's Free School for the Daughters of Impecunious Clergymen after she revealed to Scotland Yard that her headmistress had embezzled funds intended for improvement of the croquet field. This gave Mrs. Poirot even more time to devote to what would become a far better training ground for her, the observation of the daily comings and goings of her neighbors in St. Mary Mead, people so devious that she was later able, when bored with her knitting and jumble sales, to make short shrift of crimes committed not only in St. Mary Mead but also throughout Britain, the Caribbean, Africa and the Middle East.

Mr. Poirot received his master's degree in criminology from the Pierre Pasteux School of Detection in Antwerp. While still on the stage of the auditorium to receive his diploma and mongrammed pair of handcuffs, he spotted a pickpocket at work in the second row of dignitaries in the auditorium, and he leaped down, retrieved the watch, arrested the felon, and, amid great and sustained applause, received his first medal and an immediate appointment as senior inspector with the Belgian National Police.

During World War I, while recovering from battle wounds in the English village of Styles, he put his professional skills to good effect in the solving of a local murder, and he was so gratified by the admiration of Captain John Hastings and other new friends that he remained in England, serving as a consultant to Scotland Yard and also private individuals in need of his unique services.

Mr. and Mrs. Poirot met at Harrod's, where

he had gone to purchase a jar of mustache wax and she, expecting a visit from her old friend Lady Selena Hazy, to put in a supply of black currant buns. In their respective departments of the huge emporium, each happened to apprehend a shoplifter, and was then requested by a store detective to give formal evidence in the security office on the fourth floor, located just down the aisle from a display of better coronets and coronation robes. There, despite their confirmed bachelorhood and spinsterhood, they fell in love while comparing their methods of detection.

They will honeymoon in Edinburgh just as soon as they solve the mystery of the disappearance somewhere between London and Edinburgh of The Flying Scotsman, the only train that serves their favorite variety of porridge and kippers.

GRAND HOTEL

ELISAVETA ALEXANDROVNA GRUSINKAYA AND BARON FRITZ GAIGERN

In the Liebeslied Room of the Grand Hotel in Berlin, two of its distinguished guests, Elisaveta Alexandrova Grusinkaya, the talented and neurotic daughter of Alexander Ivanovitch and Varvara Maximova Grusinkay of Washington Heights in New York City and formerly of St. Petersburg (now Leningrad) in Russia (now the Union of Soviet Socialist Republics), was married yesterday to Baron Fritz Gaigern, a son of the late Baron Wilhelm Frederick and the late Baroness Marika Gaigern of Saxony. Father Hans Xavier Wingler, one of the four chaplains affiliated with the prestigious hotel during its annual upsurge in June weddings, officiated at the private ceremony. It was attended mostly by fellow guests with whom the bride and groom had become acquainted in the bar, gambling casino, or in the waiting room of Dr. Felix Obermeyer, its attendant psychoanalyst.

The bride, 37, studied with Madame Olga

Stepinskaya at the Mirov Ballet School for Exceptionally Gifted Children in St. Petersburg, and she and her classmate Anna Pavlova made joint debuts in a production of *Swan Lake* that was praised by connoisseurs and evoked twelve curtain calls and even more bouquets of long-stemmed Russian Beauty roses. Since the revolution in her homeland she has been prima ballerina with the Dresden Ballet Company, but after an ankle injury in *Les Sylphides* that has affected her pirouettes and even her raison d'etre, she is taking a leave of absence during which she will head the training school of her ballet company. The impecunious Baron Gaigern, whom she once discovered in her suite, where he had come unannounced to, allegedly, admire her famous pearls and her even more famous aura of sophistication and artistic excellence, has been a Brandenburg Gate of strength to her during this inevitable period of transition in the career of all great prima ballerinas.

The Baron Gaigern, 52, majored in artillery at the Wilhelm Maximilian Military Academy in Potsdam, and after serving with unusual distinction in the war, and receiving four Iron Crosses, was discharged with the rank of major. He never fully recovered from a head wound suffered in the Battle of Chateau-Thierry, and from time to time, succumbing to the both moral and physical after-effects of his lesion, he has engaged in what has been construed by his victims as antisocial behavior. Only last week, driven by what his distinguished neurologist, Professor Dr. Maxim Grundlich of the Kaiser Wilhelm Hospital in Hamburg, once diagnosed as a prefrontal occlusion with complication of the third synapse, he decided to purloin a wallet from the room of a fellow guest at the Grand Hotel, a ruthless businessman named Bruno Preysing. Fortunately, he first visited the bar for a stiff cognac, and there he met Samuel Seltzer, a Hollywood producer who is planning a spectacular, all-star motion picture about the long-lost Crown Princess Anastasia of Russia. The Baron and the Crown Princess had been distant cousins and also playmates in their youth, and Mr. Seltzer immediately signed the Baron to a four-year contract as historical consultant and script writer for the weekly salary of two thousand dollars, the equivalent of four trillion inflated marks.

Immediately after the wedding reception, one of the guests, Dr. Hermann Otternschlag, the hotel physician, who has frequently been heard to remark that "people come, people go, nothing ever happens at the Grand Hotel," was abducted by a gang of robbers in the corridor outside his office. With a gun pointed at his head, he was forced to accompany them to the gambling casino, where their notorious leader, Ludwig "Louie the Swine" Kellermann, had been shot in the abdomen by a security guard during an attempted holdup. While Dr. Otternschlag was still removing bullets from his unscheduled patient, a squad of elite police, led by Chief Inspector Christian von Stolling of the Unter der Linden Precinct, burst into the crowded casino. Reluctant to use their guns and risk harming innocent VIPs and their mistresses, the police released instead their containers of tear gas at the gangsters, their leader and, unfortunately, Dr. Otternschlag. As he lapsed into unconsciousness, the doctor announced his immediate retirement as hotel physician of the Grand Hotel, and added, "People come, people go, too much happens at the Grand Hotel."

TITANIC

ROSE DEWITT BUKATER AND JACK DAWSON

Rose DeWitt Bukater and Jack Dawson were married Saturday evening in the Beaux-Arts Court of the Brooklyn Museum. The ceremony was performed by the bride's dear friend and benefactor, the Rev. J. Jameson Brockhurst, pastor of the Bedford Street Unitarian Church in Sheffield, England. Until 1920, the Rev. Brockhurst was an able bodied seaman on the RMS *Carpathia*, famed for its heroic rescue of Miss Bukater and hundreds of other survivors of the *Titanic* disaster on April 15, 1912.

The bride, 27, is the daughter of the late Ruth and Randolph DeWitt Bukater of Philadelphia and Newport. Though moderately wealthy, they had long felt socially inferior to bridge and golf partners at their country club, and had wanted Rose, against her strong wishes, to marry Caledon Hockley, an up and coming steel magnate. Mrs. Bukater considered Rose too nubile to waste her time in a traditional school, and had enrolled her at fifteen in Lady Hamilton's Charm

School, located on the ultra-upscale section of the Main Line. Sure enough, within weeks of her graduation magna cum laude, she found herself engaged to Mr. Hockley and traveling from Southampton in England back to Philadelphia with him and her mother.

The groom, 30, is the son of Daisy Swirl and Mike Dawson of Highgate in London. Miss Swirl is a longtime barmaid at The Ever-Welcome Arms, a pub popular with artists, among them U.S.-British painter John Singer Sargent until his profitable portraits of Madame X and other gentry enabled him to transfer his patronage to the American Bar at the Savoy Hotel. Mr. Dawson sells vintage attire, including bowlers and deerstalkers, at the flea market in Camden Town.

Inspired by patrons of his mother, the groom took up sidewalk painting, but upon winning a lottery that offered him a 3rd class passage to Philadelphia on the *Titanic*, he packed up his equipment and rushed down to the docks. Young and ambitious, he was not deterred by warnings that the sidewalks of Philadelphia and other American cities were covered not with gold but with chewing gum that would mar his compositions, whether the subjects be British or American.

Once at sea, Rose was so distraught by the machinations of her mother and Caledon that she fled their presence and considered leaping into the sea until Jack appeared from his lowly 3rd class quarters and was able to change her mind about living and the possibility of finding true love. Within the hour, she found it in him, and he in her, but any relationship at all between them was repugnant to her mother and her detested fiancé, who framed Jack for the theft of Heart of the Ocean, his valuable necklace. When the *Titanic* struck an iceberg, and its sinking appeared inevitable, Caledon saw this as a chance to separate the lovers, and he lied and said that he had arranged for their rescue. But he intended to rescue only Rose. They were separated, and then reunited, and then separated again. Eventually, a lifeboat took Rose to the RMS *Carpathia*, a vessel that had sped to the area. She believed Jack dead, and vowed to marry no other man, and especially not Calderon, who later committed suicide.

Early in the ill-fated voyage, when Jack was informed that the decks and floors of a luxury liner were not a London sidewalk and that he could not practice his art, he had fashioned a sturdy easel from discarded lumber. The easel kept him afloat until he was picked up by a fishing boat returning to Cape Cod. Because Rose believed Jack to have drowned, and he in turn believed her, if still alive, to have married Caledon, he considered it futile for him, a pauper, to attempt to find her.

Ten years later, in 1922, by now a spokesman for a manufacturer of fine chalks and crayons, he visited the Brooklyn Museum to lecture art students and visitors about his products, the preference of, among other artists French Post-Impressionist Toulouse-Lautrec. In his audience was Rose, now a Brooklynite and employed at the public library down the block, where she had spotted a flier about his lecture.

After the wedding ceremony they visited the museum's famed collection of Egyptian statuary, which, like true love, and unlike ocean liners, is certain to survive till the end of time.

If you have enjoyed this book—and I hope that you have—please consider posting a review at Amazon.com and www.goodreads.com. Thank you.

Hy Brett

PRAISE FOR HY BRETT'S HILARIOUS SATIRE OF RIGHT-WING THINK-TANK REPORTS

A SECRET REPORT TO THE TRUE AMERICAN FAITH SOCIETY

Senior Citizens and Their Threat to America

"[Hy Brett,] you are indeed a fine satirical writer."

> Joyce Appleby, Professor Emerita of History, UCLA; Past-president of The Organization of American Historians and The American Historical Association. Author of *Shores of Knowledge*

"This is a must-read book for everyone, not only seniors, beautifully researched and eloquently written with tongue-in-cheek. It will make you laugh and it will make you angry! Best of all, it will make you vigilant."

> Kay Williams, author of *The Matryoshka Murders*

"This is wit at its best! Like Jonathan Swift's satirical, *A Modest Proposal* that suggests a way for children not to be a burden to their poor parents, Hy Brett's A SECRET REPORT offers up a simple solution on what to do with the expanding aging population—they should 'move on.' His reasoning: Medicaid is overloaded, children and grandchildren are pressed for time and resources, and senior citizens are taking a toll on civilization.... [R]eaders...who appreciate satire within the climate of political and not-so-political problems, will laugh and be amazed at Brett's audacity and sense of humor. A SECRET REPORT shouldn't be kept a secret for readers who appreciate clever, biting satire."

> Constance Walker, author of *In Time* and *The Shimmering Stones of Winter's Light*

"[A SECRET REPORT] is all too telling. As an Irishman, I am very receptive to Swiftian satire. The book moves with umph...."

> Alan Astro, Professor of Modern Languages and Literature, Trinity University. Author of *Understanding Samuel Beckett*

"Satire is one of the most difficult forms of comedic writing and Hy Brett has mastered it completely. A SECRET REPORT takes a serious subject, the growing longevity of senior citizens and their increased cost to the taxpayer, and turns it on its head with a 'solution' that's bold and witty and, because it is so well researched, thoroughly engaging. Using the device of a fictional think-tank report on the possibilities of the 'Senior Growth and Opportunity Act,' Brett considers all of the governmental and other mechanisms that might be utilized to convince seniors to do the right thing and reach a star-spangled ending. Amusing and at the same time heartfelt. I loved it and laughed out loud more times than I can count."

Jean Arbeiter, author of *Marilyn, The Prequel*